# The Logical Approach to Chess

Max Euwe · M. Blaine
J. F. S. Rumble

Dover Publications, Inc.
NEW YORK

This Dover edition, first published in 1982, is an unabridged republication of the work originally published by Sir Isaac Pitman & Sons, Ltd.,
London, in 1958. The present edition is published by special arrangement
with Pitman Publishing Ltd., 39 Parker Street, Kingsway, London
SW6 6SG, England.

Manufactured in the United States of America
Dover Publications, Inc.
180 Varick Street
New York, N.Y. 10014


**Library of Congress Cataloging in Publication Data**

Euwe, Max, 1901-
     The logical approach to chess.

     Reprint. Originally published: London: I. Pitman, 1958.
     1. Chess. I. Blaine, M. II. Rumble, J.F.S. III. Title.
GV1445.E819   1982                     794.1'2                     82-7474
     ISBN 0-486-24353-2 (pbk.)                                     AACR2

# PREFACE

## by

## Dr. M. Euwe

Even on a cursory first inspection of the original draft manuscript of this book I was greatly impressed by its dispassionate approach and its very systematic method of presentation. Beginning with a number of simple maxims of military strategy, the book proceeds to present and elaborate very clearly the fundamental principles of chess. The choice of examples, for the most part taken from the games of players who were not chess masters, is an experiment that must be considered extremely successful.

In view of the outstanding qualities that emerged even on a first reading, I was greatly attracted by the authors' suggestion that I should collaborate with them. Yet at first I hesitated, for I felt some scruples because my share of the labour would not be in proportion to that of the other authors. Eventually, however, the scales were turned by my realization that I should be able to subscribe to every word of the text in its final form. I therefore willingly fell in with the wishes of those who are now my fellow authors, in order that I might express in a practical manner my admiration for their achievement.

M. E.

# PREFACE

by

M. BLAINE AND J. F. S. RUMBLE

DURING the last war, while serving with the R.A.F. in Ceylon we spent our leaves with Mr. C. E. V. Ryan, a tea planter and a keen chessplayer.

He told us that the chess books he had read were either too elementary or too advanced for him, and he had been unable to find anything which bridged the gap between them.

From our talks with him came the idea of this book—to begin with a study of the board and men and then, step by step, to build up logically a plan and method of playing chess. At the same time it was designed to give the reader a sound basis from which he could begin to understand the play of the chess masters.

We showed the completed manuscript to two chess friends, D. B. Scott and J. D. Soloman, and later to the then British Champion R. J. Broadbent, to all of whom we are most grateful for numerous helpful suggestions.

During the Hastings Congress of 1949–50 we showed the manuscript to Dr. Euwe, whose play and logical writings on the game we had always admired.

We were naturally delighted when he at once showed keen interest in the book, and undertook to revise it for us.

The present book is thus the result of the combined efforts of the three of us, and a Dutch Edition has already appeared in Holland and Belgium.

M. B.

J. F. S. R.

# CONTENTS

CHAPTER IV

THE END-GAME

CHAPTER V

THE THEORY IN ACTION

# CHAPTER I

# The Centre and its Implications

## THE FIELD OF BATTLE

THE similarity between a game of chess and a military battle is a remarkable one, and much can be learnt by comparing the two. Everybody knows that chess is a type of warfare—indeed, that is supposed to be the origin of the game—yet how often is this knowledge put to practical use?

For instance, let us suppose a military battle about to commence. There are two main factors each opposing Commander-in-Chief must consider. They are—

(1) The field of battle.

(2) The men under his command.

It very often happens, however, that little or no consideration is given to the field of battle—the chessboard—when learning chess. It is regarded merely as a medium on which to move the men. Yet who can really understand the nature of the tasks confronting him in a battle who does not know every detail of the terrain over which the battle must be fought?

The field of battle in chess is a square. Examine the square here illustrated. Suppose you were asked to take up a position inside that square in order to retrieve a ball which would be

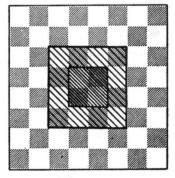

*Diagram 1*

thrown somewhere inside that square *after* you had taken up your position.

Where would you stand in order to have the best chance of getting the ball in the shortest time no matter where it fell?

The answer is clear. The CENTRE of the square, since that is the point equidistant from the four corners.

In the case of a chessboard this would be one of the four centre squares.

That occupation of the centre of a (limited) battlefield will give you the maximum possible manœuvrability is often forgotten when the field is thick with ominous-looking enemy men creeping down the flanks! Think of the last game of chess you played. Did these central squares stand out in your mind throughout the whole game? If not, then already, by this study of the board, you have learnt one of the most important fundamental chess truths.

From the aspect of manœuvrability, *the centre of the board has an importance greatly exceeding the flanks or corners.*

Against an opponent, however "naturally" strong he may be, who is not aware of the value of a central position, but instead launches violent and even spectacular wing attacks, your knowledge of this fact, and the subsequent centralized position of your forces will give you a distinct advantage in dealing with any situation which may arise.

Examine the board again. Suppose you had a vital treasure, relatively immobile in the corner *B*. Rather than have them in the centre, would it not be better, you might ask, to arrange your forces in a semi-circle round that corner *B*? You are then safe against any outflanking movement. The most frequent application of this idea in chess occurs in an attack against your castled King.

The arrows in diagram 2 indicate forces attacking a King encircled by its own men.

In certain circumstances it may be essential for your forces to move over to the side in defence of the King, but in this case, if they are in the centre of the board, their greater mobility will facilitate this operation.

In addition, a strong force in the centre will harass the enemy's lines of communication to the flank he is attacking, and a full scale or divisionary counter attack may relieve the pressure to a greater extent than a static defence.

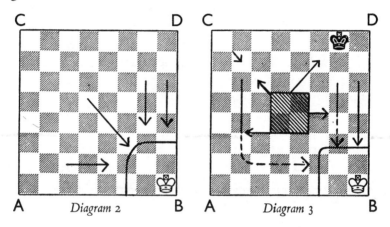

Diagram 2              Diagram 3

Diagram 3 shows how a strong central position can break up the same attacking forces and, in addition, threaten the attacker's own defensive position.

Our study of the battlefield, as applied to chess, has thus revealed that although there are no artificial barriers, tank traps or similar obstructions, there is one natural strongpoint—*the centre of the board.*

## VALUE AND EFFECTIVENESS OF THE PIECES

It is clear that some of the chess pieces are more valuable than others—that a Queen, for instance, is more valuable than a Bishop. Why is this so?

Both Queen and Bishop can move any number of squares diagonally across the board, but in addition the Queen has the power to move any number of squares along the files and ranks, which the Bishop cannot do. From this we can easily see that the value of a piece lies in its *power of movement*, and only in its power of movement.

There are no exceptions to this rule. The Knight's unique power of passing over other pieces, the sideways taking of the pawn, and even the capturing "en passant" of that piece are all only functions of their power of movement.

But doesn't the power of capture influence the value of a piece? *No!* If, for instance, a Knight were not allowed by the rules of chess to capture a Queen, then their powers of capture would have a great bearing on the value of each piece, but this is not so.

It is naturally difficult to arrive at an exact assessment of the value of the pieces, since so much depends on where each one is situated on the field of battle, and the general position of the game. It is, however, essential to have some good idea of their relative values, particularly when considering whether to make (or avoid) an exchange.

Given an equal position, therefore, and with each piece taken as having its full powers of movement, the following table of relative values has been found convenient and accurate by the authors—

A QUEEN is equal to TWO ROOKS.

A MINOR PIECE, i.e. a Knight or Bishop is equal to THREE PAWNS.

A ROOK is equal to a MINOR PIECE, plus ONE PAWN AND A HALF,

i.e. a Rook is stronger than a minor piece and one pawn, but is at a disadvantage against a minor piece and two pawns.

*Note.* A Knight is equal to a Bishop, but two Bishops are a very strong weapon, generally preferable to a Knight and Bishop or two Knights, owing to their two-colour long-range action.

It must be emphasized that these values are true only when conditions are equal, but then should be very carefully borne in mind when contemplating an exchange of pieces. Relative positions of the opposing forces do, of course, affect the value of the pieces, and it is often wise to exchange a more valuable piece for a less valuable one in order, for example, to effect a mate, or gain some particular advantage.

Let us consider now in more detail some aspects of the effectiveness of the pieces.

(1) The pieces should be placed so as to attain their maximum manœuvrability.

The truth of this statement is self-evident, since we already know that the value of the pieces is dependent entirely on their powers of movement. A piece placed where its power of movement is restricted loses a lot of its effectiveness, and is therefore not giving its full value—in fact it will not *be* so valuable *so long as it remains in that position.*

(2) Always bear in mind the latent power of each piece.

Because a piece is at the moment very limited in its manœuvrability, that does not mean that two moves hence it will not be exerting its maximum pressure.

Take a Knight for example. Where would you place a Knight on the board so that it obtained its maximum powers of movement? Somewhere in the centre of the board, in this case on one of the sixteen centre squares. In the case of the Bishop, its maximum powers

Diagram 4

of movement occur only when it is on one of the four centre squares.

In the centre of the board (diagram 4, page 5) a Knight can move on to any one of eight squares. At the side of the board it exerts pressure on only four squares, and therefore loses 50 per cent of its intrinsic value *while it remains* in that position. In the corner of the board it commands only two squares, and has lost 75 per cent of its full value.

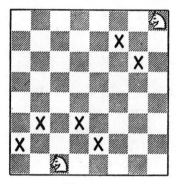

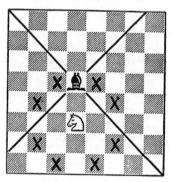

*Diagram 5*                    *Diagram 6*

Note from diagram 6 that the Bishop has a potential thirteen squares on to which it can move, as against eight for the Knight, but against this the Knight could threaten to capture eight different pieces, whereas the Bishop would at most be able to threaten four.

In the case of all the pieces except the Rook, they are most effective when placed centrally. In the case of the Rook, it controls the same number of squares wherever it may be on the board.

## Conclusions

Concerning the value and effectiveness of the pieces, we have come to the following conclusions—

(1) The value of a piece is dependent entirely on its power

of movement. Indeed, the value of a piece *is* its power of movement.

(2) The power of capturing possessed by a piece is merely a function of that power of movement, since any piece can take any opposing piece.

(3) A good player, therefore, will place his pieces where they control the greatest number of squares, and consequently give of their maximum value.

These considerations being equal, the relative value of the pieces is shown by the table previously given.

*Note.* One word of caution is needed here. Remember that you are the Commander-in-Chief, and *all* the men are at your disposal. Thus it is not enough merely to place each individual piece where it controls its maximum squares. All are part of a team, and it is the team as a whole that must control the largest number of squares possible, and it may well be necessary to curtail the activities of one piece to enhance the value of another. Thus, for example, a Bishop might be employed only to maintain and protect a well-placed Knight or vice versa.

## CONTROL OF THE CENTRE—PHYSICAL AND DISTANT CONTROL

We now know that the centre of the board forms a natural strategic vantage-point. If your opponent is unaware of the importance of the centre squares, it may be possible for you to occupy them with your pieces, in which case you will possess the following advantages—

(1) It is from the central position that forces can be deployed most effectively and rapidly both in attack and defence.

From the centre there are eight possible directions in which the forces as a whole can operate. On the other hand, forces disposed to one side of the board can fan out in only five directions, those in the corner in only three. Again, if one's forces are disposed on one side of the board and an attack develops on the other side, it would take much longer to switch them over to counter this attack than if they had been centrally placed.

(2) The mobility of all the pieces (except the Rooks) is increased when they are placed in the centre of the board, which further increases the advantage of a central position.

The centre of the board should, therefore, constitute the pivot of one's plan of campaign and every available means should be

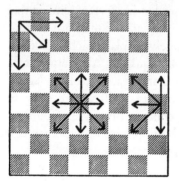

employed to exercise control over it. Though control by occupation does reap the greatest rewards, if your opponent is also "centrally minded," he may make it impossible or far too dangerous for you to do this, at least in the early stages of the game.

It is, nevertheless, still of the utmost importance to try to control the centre, and such con-

*Diagram 7*

trol can be exercised with pieces operating some distance from the four centre squares.

In diagram 8 both sides have equal control which is being exercised by the pawns in the centre, the Knights fairly near, and the Bishops which are some distance away.

There are occasions when actual occupation may even hinder the general mobility and efficiency of your supporting pieces behind the central squares.

For example, in diagram 9 the centre square (White's Q4) is physically occupied by a pawn. Were the white pawn not at Q4, however, not only would the Queen, Bishop or Knight be able to move to Q4, but the long diagonal would be opened up for the Bishop. Although any piece may take any opposing piece, trial by court-martial and "shooting" of one's own men for sabotage is not allowed. Consequently, if your pieces become blocked in the centre (particularly if they are relatively immobile pawns) it may be impossible for you to get them out of the way and thus release your supporting pieces for action. You may

Diagram 8              Diagram 9

then find yourself with your forces in the position of confusion, which occurred in the ranks of Tuscany when

"Those behind cried 'FORWARD'
"And those in front cried 'BACK'."

Early in the game it is often impossible to place your pieces on any of the central squares. They are too liable to be driven off by hostile pawns, and in any case the number of squares in the centre available for occupation will be limited by your own pawns, as well as those of your opponent.

Another disadvantage of attempting a too early occupation of the centre with pieces is that they are liable to be captured by the opponent's pieces, whereas say a Bishop at Kt2, though still exercising central pressure, is safely tucked away in the heart of your own camp, and thus very difficult to capture.

You must usually be content in the opening stages of the game to exert pressure on the centre from a distance, e.g. by Knights on B3, and Bishops at Kt2 or B4. But always have the occupation of the centre as your aspiration, and if, later in the game, the opportunity occurs to place your pieces centrally, then seize it with open arms.

# CHAPTER II

# Opening Theory

## THE FUNDAMENTALS OF OPENINGS

THERE are many different types of openings. Many of these have queer foreign-sounding names, calculated to terrorize any chess player. Yet, in spite of their wide diversity, all openings have a common basis. Until this common basis is fully understood it is both useless and unwise to delve into the intricate mass of "set" openings.

The basis of beginning a game of chess is built up of a number of factors. The most important of these factors are given below as fundamentals of openings. The less important are given as advice but nevertheless even these should not be departed from lightly.

The fundamentals are—

(1) The quickest central development of all the pieces.

(2) Harmony of development.

Remember that all the pieces are units of a team, and must therefore be developed in harmony, and not act independently. For example—

|   |   |   |   |
|---|---|---|---|
| 1 | P–K4 | | P–K4 |
| 2 | Kt–KB3 | | B–Q3 (diagram 10) |

Here the Bishop is developed, but not in harmony, because by blocking its own Queen's pawn it retards development of the other Bishop.

(3) Castling.

This not only puts the King into a position of safety, but brings the Rook into action.

In diagram 11 the Rooks are connected and if need be they can bring pressure to bear on the centre.

*Diagram 10*

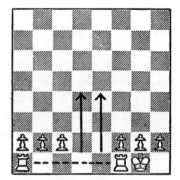

*Diagram 11*

### ADVICE CONCERNING DEVELOPMENT

(1) *Avoid losing a tempo.*

A Tempo is a TIME-MOVE unit, the time being measured against your opponent's progress.

For example—

(a)          1   P–K4                    P–K4

The position is even and White has the move.

(b)          1   P–K3                    P–K4
             2   P–K4

The position is still even, but now Black has the move. White has therefore lost ONE TEMPO. A loss of tempo is not merely a "waste of time," or waste of a move, it is only a waste (or gain) compared with your opponent's progress, since after

(c)     1  P–K3          P–K3
        2  P–K4          P–K4

The position is again even and White still has the move and thus has not lost a tempo. But he has certainly wasted time by accomplishing in two moves what could be done in one.

(2) *Do not bring the Queen too early into the game.*

For example—

        1  P–K4          P–Q4
        2  P×P           Q×P
        3  Kt–QB3

The Knight now attacks the Queen and gains a tempo at once, since the Queen must move again, and White can develop another piece.

        3  ...           Q–K4 *ch*

A check which serves no useful purpose is better held in reserve.

        4  B–K2          Kt–B3
        5  Kt–B3

This now attacks the Queen again, and gains yet another tempo.

If the position (diagram 12) is now analysed, after only five moves on either side we can see that White has already by far the superior game, for not only has he developed three minor pieces to Black's one, but he is in a position to castle. His

*Diagram 12*

command over the centre of the board is superior and he will have soon completed his development, while Black still has teething troubles.

Examine the following opening—

| 1 | P–K4 | P–QB4 |
|---|------|-------|
| 2 | Kt–KB3 | Kt–QB3 |
| 3 | P–Q4 | P×P |
| 4 | Kt×P | P–Q3 |

The authors were once asked "Why does not Black play 4 ... Kt×Kt, since it compels 5 Q×Kt, and an early exit of White's Queen?"

Examine the position again after Q×Kt.

*Diagram* 13

The reader, now well acquainted with the all-important centre, will know the answer. There is now no Knight to gain tempo at the Queen's expense, but even more important—

(1) Black's remaining pieces are all in their original positions.

(2) White has occupation and complete control of the centre of the board.

(3) *Pawns in front of the castled King.*

Don't move the pawns on the side to which the King intends to castle.

Diagrams 14, 15 and 16 illustrate some of the more usual dangers which may result from moving these pawns.

*Diagram* 14. In this diagram the King's Bishop's pawn has been pushed up to drive the Knight away. This, however, has allowed Black to check with the Bishop and win a Rook for the Knight. ("Winning the Exchange.")

*Diagram* 15. Here the Rook's pawn has been played up to

keep the black Bishop from Kt5, but by bringing the Queen on to the Knight's file Black threatens B × P.

*Diagram* 16. This illustrates the weakness on the White squares following P–Kt3.

This advice is one which should be generally followed, but there are exceptions which concern the King's Knight's pawn and the King's Bishop's pawn. The Knight's pawn may be

Diagram 14

Diagram 15

played to Kt3 if it is intended to fianchetto the Bishop to Kt2, for in this position the Bishop takes the place of the displaced pawn, and indeed the formation is stronger than just the pawn at Kt2 (diagram 17).

Diagram 16

Diagram 17

The King's Bishop's pawn may be played to B4 in certain types of openings, either prior to castling or afterwards, but the weakness thus created on the diagonal, as shown in diagram 14, requires very careful handling.

The various types of openings all aim at the same end, full development of all the pieces and control of the centre.

*Until the fundamentals have been carried out no attempt should be made to embark on any other activity, however tempting that activity may appear.*

## HOW TO SELECT FROM A CHOICE OF MOVES

It is essential to have a clear idea of how to select at any stage of the game those moves which most effectively further one's plans for conducting the game. This is particularly necessary in the opening stages when there is so often a wide and varied selection of reasonable moves from which to choose.

We have already seen the fundamentals to be observed in opening play, now let us examine the opening of a game.

### 1   P–K4

This move as we have discussed earlier, strikes immediately at the centre by occupying K4 and bringing pressure to bear on Q5, and also releases the King's Bishop and the Queen for development.

### 1   ...          P–K4

Black replies with the same move *for the same reasons*, not because White has played it!

### 2   Kt–KB3

This move develops a piece centrally, attacks Black's King's pawn (by bringing pressure to bear on White's K5) and in addition challenges Black's command of his Q5, e.g. after White plays P–Q4, Black could play P×P but White's Knight could then recapture and Black's pressure on his Q5 would be neutralized. Now what is Black to play next?

He has the choice of the following possible moves—

1 P–K4, P–K4; 2 Kt–KB3

(a)                2 ...                B–Q3 (diagram 18)

This move is in opposition to the fundamental opening theory (harmony of the pieces) for it blocks the Queen's pawn and thus the Queen's Bishop

(b)                2 ...                Q–K2 (diagram 19)

Diagram 18

Diagram 19

This move blocks the King's Bishop and utilizes the Queen too early in the game.

(c)                2 ...                Q–B3

This has the same objections as Q–K2, this time blocking the central development of the King's Knight.

(d)                2 ...                P–KB3 (diagram 20)

This blocks central development of the King's Knight and opens up White's QR2–KKt8 diagonal. (See also opening advice No. 3.) The placing of a Bishop on this diagonal for instance, would make it very difficult for Black to castle (King's Rook), and would hinder his development by the pressure on his K3 and Q4.

(e)            2  ...                    P–Q4 (diagram 21)

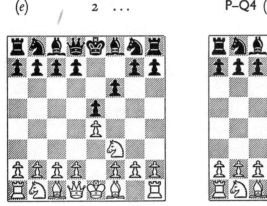

Diagram 20                    Diagram 21

This move makes a premature attempt to wrest control of the centre, since the Queen's pawn is now defended only by the Queen and after 3 P×P, Q×P White gains a tempo by 4 Kt–QB3. Black may not retake with the Queen, but instead play 3 ... P–K5.

Now analyse the position. Although this move attacks the Knight, the King's pawn no longer exerts pressure on a centre square, and apart from causing White temporary embarrassment, leaves him with a pawn up and still the one piece developed against none for Black.

(f)            2  ...                    P–KB4 (diagram 22)

This counter attack is very hazardous for Black, since, as indicated in the diagram, it opens up dangerous diagonals (as in the case of P–KB3) and neither develops a piece, nor releases another piece for development.

(g)            2 ...                    **P–Q3** (diagram 23)

This move restricts the King's Bishop, but releases the Queen's Bishop for development. Therefore, apart from being passively inclined it can be considered as satisfactory.

*Diagram 22*

*Diagram 23*

(h)            2 ...                    **Kt–QB3** (diagram 24)

This possesses none of the disadvantages so far mentioned. It develops a piece centrally, defends the pawn and reasserts Black's pressure on his Q5, which has now two black pieces bearing on it against one of White's.

*Diagram 24*

*Diagram 25*

(i)                2 ...                    Kt–KB3 (diagram 25)

This move does not defend the pawn, but it does develop a piece centrally and attacks a pawn of equal value (a centre pawn). It also challenges White's control of his Q5 by bringing pressure to bear on that square.

CONCLUSION

It will be seen from the foregoing analysis how the selection should be thought out. In this example the first four moves should obviously be rejected and the last three are all playable. Moves (e) and (f) are hazardous. The objections to them have been pointed out, and although they are sometimes adopted by Chess Masters (even Chess Masters must be allowed their Poetic Licence) we do not advise the reader to follow suit.

From the analysis will also be clearly seen the reason for the frequency that occurs of the opening moves after 1 P–K4, P–K4; of 2 Kt–KB3, Kt–QB3.

It might be asked, "Are there not occasions when it is permissible, or advisable, to violate the fundamentals in the opening?" We advise the reader, at this stage, *never* to do so, except, of course, to take material advantage *in the event (only) of an obvious error or oversight* on the part of his opponent. For example: after 1 P–K4, P–K4; 2 Kt–KB3, Q–Kt4? we advise the reader to play 3 Kt×Q, even at the expense of speedier development! But we would observe that 3 P–Q4, is aesthetically better!! (if 3 ... P×P; 4 B×Q) developing another piece without loss of tempo.

### VARIOUS WAYS OF ACHIEVING THE SAME OBJECT

We have already seen that the various methods of opening are merely different ways of achieving the same object.

Now set up the white pieces only on the board in their original positions, and try to discover for yourself different and distinct positions in which the pieces are fully developed in accordance with the principles and advice we have learnt. To do this, move each piece not more than once, and take down your methods separately as in the following example—

1 P–K4, 2 Kt–KB3, 3 B–B4, 4 P–Q4, 5 B–K3, 6 P–QB3, 7 QKt–Q2, 8 O–O.

Now try to discover for yourself at least two more methods different from above. Then compare them with the follow-

*Diagram 26*

ing examples, but remember that it will be much more satisfactory, and give you additional confidence if you can discover them or similar ones for yourself.

Now examine the diagrams below, illustrating various methods of development.

*Diagram 27*

*Diagram 28*

Satisfy yourself that these examples fulfil the conditions of full and correct development, testing them and your own positions against the following questions—

(1) Is every minor piece developed?

(2) Has White castled?

(3) Is each developed piece bearing directly or indirectly on the centre?

(4) Have the Rooks free movement on the back rank?

Exactly the same principles apply when opening with the black pieces, but since your opponent will have the first move, *your choice will be restricted* according to the mode of development adopted by White. Apart from that, you can develop, within

*Diagram 29*

the limits imposed upon you, in whatever way you choose.

For example, amongst other choices White can *always* open with P–K4, P–Q4, or P–QB4, but in this event Black's choice is restricted. If White, say, plays 1 P–K4, Black can play in reply

*Diagram 30*

*Diagram 31*

1 P–K4, or P–QB4, but would be unwise to reply 1 P–Q4, because of White's reply 2 P×P, and if the Queen retakes we

have 3 Kt–QB3, with a gain in tempo as in the example previously given.

In the same way, if White opens 1 P–Q4, it would be unwise to adopt 1 P–K4, in reply. This restricting influence will, of course, make itself felt in the subsequent moves as well, and Black can often likewise restrict White's choice later.

The following examples and Diagrams 30, 31, and 32 show various methods of development particularly applicable to Black. The White pawns indicate White's first moves.

The reader should satisfy himself that these examples similarly

*Diagram 32*

conform with the principles. These examples of development for the white and black pieces form the basis for most of the weird-sounding openings splashed around in chess books and magazines.

Next time your opponent with a knowing smile tells you that his last move was Rasputin's variation in the Rimsky-Korsakov Defence, do not grow pale and resign the game. He is probably only developing a piece centrally!

## EXAMPLES OF THE VARIOUS METHODS OF DEVELOPMENT IN ACTUAL PLAY

Even with the white pieces, a method of development can be, and often is, interfered with by an opponent.

When this happens it is necessary to adapt the method chosen to the play of one's opponent, but by playing always in accordance with the principles the reader will not find this too difficult.

In order to give some idea as to how such modification can be carried out, examples are given below.

In each instance a mode of development, as shown in the previous diagrams, is selected and two examples are given—one in which the plan is to all intents and purposes carried out without undue trouble from the opposing forces, and the second in which it is not possible to do so.

Where this happens, though the original plan has to be modified or even radically altered, it can be seen that the resultant development still conforms with the basic principles.

*Example One*

Let us suppose the reader has the white pieces and decides that he will develop so as to reach the dispositions as shown in diagram 26. The game might go as follows—

| | White | Black |
|---|---|---|
| 1 | P–K4 | P–K4 |
| 2 | Kt–KB3 | Kt–QB3 |
| 3 | B–B4 | B–B4 |
| 4 | P–B3 | Kt–B3 |
| 5 | P–Q3 | P–Q3 |
| 6 | B–K3 | B–Kt3 |

Were Black to exchange Bishops at this stage, after 6 ... B×B; 7 P×B; White would benefit. He would have an extra pawn strengthening his centre, and after castling, the Rook would have potential manœuvrability and pressure on the King's Bishop file.

| | | |
|---|---|---|
| 7 | QKt–Q2 | Kt–K2 |
| 8 | P–Q4 | O–O |
| 9 | O–O | |

and White has achieved his planned dispositions.

On the other hand the game might equally well have gone as under—

| | | |
|---|---|---|
| 1 | P–K4 | P–K4 |
| 2 | Kt–KB3 | Kt–QB3 |

| 3 | B–B4 | Kt–KB3 |
|---|------|--------|
| 4 | P–Q3 | P–Q4   |

After this move White's plan must clearly be modified.

| 5 | P×P  | Kt×P  |
|---|------|-------|
| 6 | O–O  | B–K2  |
| 7 | R–K1 |       |

White further modifies his plan in order to take advantage of a weakness that has arisen in Black's position on his K4.

The reader should always remember that it is not sufficient to follow slavishly any preconceived plan, however good in itself. The consequence of every move made by the opponent should be carefully examined, and advantage taken of any weakness in his position. This must be done by modification in the disposition of your forces, and *not by abandoning development.*

*Example Two*

In this example White selects diagram 28.

| 1 | P–Q4   | P–Q4   |
|---|--------|--------|
| 2 | P–QB4  | P–K3   |
| 3 | Kt–QB3 | Kt–KB3 |
| 4 | Kt–B3  | QKt–Q2 |
| 5 | P×P    | P×P    |
| 6 | B–B4   | P–B3   |
| 7 | P–K3   | B–K2   |
| 8 | B–Q3   | O–O    |
| 9 | O–O    |        |

White again gets his development without discomfort. But after

| 1 | P–Q4 | P–QB4 |
|---|------|-------|

White must immediately modify his plan, and the game may go

| 2 | P–Q5 |
|---|------|

Black's first move makes a direct challenge in the centre. If White plays 2 P×P, Black could, if desired, immediately regain the pawn by Q–R4 *ch*, and would then have gained a white centre pawn for a more distant one of his own. White does not wish to move *away* from the centre, or allow this exchange.

|   |       |        |
|---|-------|--------|
| 2 | ...   | P–K4   |
| 3 | P–K4  | P–Q3   |
| 4 | B–Q3  | P–QR3  |
| 5 | P–QR4 |        |

Black with his last move was threatening a flank attack with P–QKt4, and so White must postpone further development for a move in order to counter this threat.

|    |        |        |
|----|--------|--------|
| 5  | ...    | Kt–K2  |
| 6  | Kt–K2  | Kt–Kt3 |
| 7  | Kt–R3  | B–K2   |
| 8  | Kt–QB4 | O–O    |
| 9  | O–O    | Kt–Q2  |
| 10 | B–Q2   |        |

White still has correct, though considerably modified, development.

### Example Three

We will now consider an example in which the reader has the black pieces, and chooses, after White's 1 P–K4 to play along the lines of diagram 32.

*Uninterrupted*

|   |        |        |
|---|--------|--------|
| 1 | P–K4   | P–K3   |
| 2 | P–Q4   | P–Q4   |
| 3 | Kt–QB3 | Kt–KB3 |
| 4 | B–KKt5 | B–K2   |
| 5 | P–K5   | KKt–Q2 |

| 6 | B × B | Q × B |
|---|-------|-------|
| 7 | P–B4 | P–QR3 |
| 8 | Kt–B3 | P–QB4 |
| 9 | P × P | Kt × P |
| 10 | B–Q3 | Kt–QB3 |
| 11 | Q–Q2 | B–Q2 |

*Interrupted*

| 1 | P–K4 | P–K3 |
|---|------|------|
| 2 | P–Q4 | P–Q4 |
| 3 | P × P | P × P |
| 4 | Kt–KB3 | Kt–KB3 |
| 5 | B–Q3 | B–K2 |
| 6 | Kt–B3 | P–B3 |
| 7 | B–KKt5 | B–KKt5 |

The above examples are naturally only a few of those which may occur. Every game the reader plays in future will provide further examples and practice.

## THE EVOLUTION OF CHESS STRATEGY

The reader will now be familiar with the principles underlying the various openings. The next question which may well be asked is, "What is my opponent doing all this time, while I am so busy developing in accordance with all these principles?" To answer that we must consider how chess strategy has evolved.

What is the ultimate object in a game of chess? It is the "capture" of the opposing King. How is this object to be achieved?

Chess strategy has passed through numerous stages of evolution. Originally, since the King was the ultimate object, games took the form of a direct attack against the King. Now launching an attack against the whole of an opposing force with a few quickly developed pieces is unlikely to succeed unless the opponent plays very badly, or neglects his own development and thus fails to utilize all his forces for the defence.

Thus it came to be realized that speedy development of *all* one's forces was required to conduct a successful attack against the opposing King's position. Should the opponent not also develop fully, it was possible by hurling all one's pieces into the attack, to overpower that opponent and capture his King, since you were operating with the superior (mobilized) force.

The following game, played by Paul Morphy in 1858, will illustrate the utilization of fully mobilized forces against an opponent who ignores his own development and tries to attack with a few pieces, and will provide the reader with a little light diversion.

| White (*Morphy*) | Black |
|---|---|
| 1   P–K4 | P–K4 |
| 2   Kt–KB3 | P–Q3 |
| 3   P–Q4 | B–Kt5 |
| 4   P×P | B×Kt |
| 5   Q×B | P×P |
| 6   B–QB4 | Kt–KB3 |
| 7   Q–QKt3 | Q–K2 |
| 8   Kt–B3 | |

Morphy is aware that not being fully developed, he is not yet in a position to launch an attack. Therefore, he does not consider playing the *apparently* attractive 8 Q×KtP, but presses on with his development.

| 8   . . . | P–B3 |
|---|---|
| 9   B–Kt5 | P–Kt4 ??? |

Black attacks the Bishop. He is, of course, hopelessly behind with his development while Morphy, on the other hand, is ready to castle. Small wonder that Black's puny attempt is repulsed and White's coming onslaught overwhelms him. The manner in which Morphy does this is a delight to see.

|    |               |         |
|----|---------------|---------|
| 10 | Kt×P          | P×Kt    |
| 11 | B×P *ch*      | Kt–Q2   |
| 12 | O–O–O(QR)     |         |

The final developing move is now added to the weight of the attack.

|    |     |       |
|----|-----|-------|
| 12 | ... | R–Q1  |

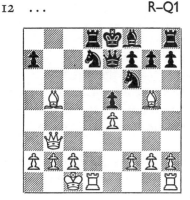

*Diagram* 33

|    |        |       |
|----|--------|-------|
| 13 | R×Kt   | R×R   |
| 14 | R–Q1   | Q–K3  |

Releasing the pinned Knight. This Knight goes out in a blaze of glory, but alas! he is only one member of a team and that team is defeated.

|    |          |       |
|----|----------|-------|
| 15 | B×R *ch* | Kt×B  |
| 16 | Q–Kt8 *ch* | Kt×Q |
| 17 | R–Q8 *mate* |    |

Every piece utilized while Black's King's Bishop and King's Rook never saw a shot fired in anger!

Full development, therefore, is required before any attempt to embark upon an attack. Gradually, however, this knowledge became the property of almost every chess player, and when both sides were fully developed a direct attack on the King usually resulted in an even exchange of pieces and an early draw —if not a reaction to the disadvantage of the attacking player.

It then became necessary, in order to carry out a successful attack, not only to achieve full development, but to occupy "strong-points" on the field of battle as well.

Now we know that the most important vantage-point is the centre of the board. When both sides are fully developed the possibility of a successful attack lies with the player who has the greater control of the centre.

When both players realize the importance of the centre, and neither side has sufficient control there to conduct a satisfactory attack, it is necessary to utilize various minor strategic "strong-points," and other tactical considerations in order to achieve an advantage.

We now return to the original question with which we opened the chapter. "What is my opponent doing while I am so busy attending to all these principles?" Roughly speaking he will be doing one of three things.

(1) Ignoring his own development and perhaps launching an attack.

(2) Developing quickly, but haphazardly.

(3) Developing in accordance with the principles, and with a view to control of the centre.

In the first case, we know an attack without full development can never succeed against an opponent who develops properly. It may be necessary to deal with such an attack before finally completing your own development—never ignore what your opponent is playing, even, if it is wrong play. However, you *know* his attack can be broken up, so discover the best way and break it up ruthlessly. Then hurry on with your own development before launching your counter-attack.

In the second case, although actual development may be equal, you will have all the advantages which accrue from a control of the centre.

In the third case, neither side may have an advantage, and so before going further, the "minor" strategical considerations must be investigated, as enumerated in the next chapter.

The reader, therefore, having arrived at the stage when he has completed development to his satisfaction, should examine with even greater care the position on the board and decide into which of the three categories his opponent's forces fall—

(1) Opponent not developed (as in the previous game).

(2) Opponent fully developed but weak centrally.

(3) Equal development and centre.

We know how to deal with the first case, and realize we are bound to have the advantage in the second. How to exploit that advantage, and how to deal with the third, belongs to the next section, "The Middle-game."

# CHAPTER III

# The Middle-Game

IT is impossible to understand the middle-game as a whole without first gaining knowledge of the parts that go to make up that whole. Thus we begin this section with an examination of all those various and diverse factors that occur with such frequency during middle-games.

First, we have the pawns, their strengths and weaknesses—in formations and as "individuals." Pawn play forms a vitally important part of this stage of the game. Then come the other "minor" strategic conceptions—powerful weapons for the use of those who understand them—open files and the seventh rank, the Knight outpost, and the art of exchanging.

All these things have been dissected out, as it were, from the body of the middle-game so that they can be the more clearly seen and understood. In reality, though, they are inseparable from the middle-game as a whole, and inseparable indeed from one another.

In breaking down these parts from the whole, extensive use has been made of "skeleton" diagrams. This term simply means that in a diagram, only the pieces relevant to the factor which is being discussed at any particular moment are included. Thus Black's King may appear on a diagram and not White's or there may be no Kings on the board at all.

May we remind the reader that these diagrams have but one object—to illustrate as clearly and economically as possible the point under discussion when the diagram appears. They are neither positions for analysis nor chess problems. No elaborate analysis will appear anywhere in this book, which is concerned only with the teaching of *principles*. General lines of play, with one or two concrete examples, may well be shown in order to show the working of a principle, but the kind of position in which "White plays and wins in twelve moves against all possibilities" does not appear.

We would ask the reader to be patient—to learn and become familiar with these essential details before worrying about the middle-game in its entirety.

*Note.* All diagrams have White playing up the board, except where it is specified otherwise.

## THE PAWNS—GENERAL CONSIDERATIONS

There are two main divisions into which the functions of pawns can be divided—dynamic and static. If we employ a military analogy again, the pawns may be either active infantrymen, engaged perhaps in leading an attack, or they may be immobile, perhaps defending an important point (e.g. a square) from a defensive "pill box" entrenchment. Though the same pawns at different times combine both dynamic and static functions, it will facilitate understanding if these two aspects are treated separately.

### THE PAWNS AS A DYNAMIC FORCE

Pawns have their own power of movement. They have the power to move forward and to attack diagonally.

(1) Pawns are generally more effective than pieces, in driving enemy pieces away from important squares.

When a piece is attacked by a pawn, unless that pawn can be captured, the piece must generally move away. When it is attacked by another piece it can often be defended, and thus need not move away from the square it is occupying.

Consider the example which follows.

In this position the Knight, attacked by the pawn, must move even though the other Knight can be brought up to support it.

A Knight being more valuable than a pawn, an exchange would react to White's advantage.

If, however, this Knight were attacked by a Bishop, the other Knight could support it, and thus it need not move, an exchange leading to no material loss.

*Diagram 34*

(2) Pawns are frequently of the utmost value in the vanguard of an attack against an opponent's position.

The task of the pawns in an attack is generally that of breaking up the opposing defences and thus allowing the pieces behind access to the objective. An attack might be defeated by having a superior force to deal with the attacking pieces *after* the position has been opened up. This can be done, but in making his attack the aggressor usually reckons on having superior forces in that area, so this method is the exception rather than the rule. So in most cases the defender will rely on holding up the attacking pawns and preventing, if he can, the opening up of the position.

The guiding principle, therefore, in moving pawns into the attack must be to *maintain their mobility*. Before making each pawn move, the attacker should be very careful to see that by such a move, he does not allow the defending pawns, or pieces, to move in such a way as to prevent further advance by his own pawn-force.

Maintaining pawns in positions where they retain their potential mobility has also a great psychological advantage. The defender will always have to be on the alert, since he cannot be sure *which*, if any, of the mobile pawns will advance next.

Let us consider some examples of pawns in attack to illustrate these points.

*Attacking in the Centre*

This position in diagram 35 shows opposing pawns in the centre. White is in a position to play 1 P-Q4. If Black replies 1 ... P×P, then after 2 P×P, White has improved his control of the central squares, and his pawns remain mobile. If Black refrains from taking, he may have to remain in a state of tension, while White regroups forces for a further advance.

*Diagram 35*

*Attacks on a Wing*

In the position in diagram 36 White has mobile pawns but Black has not. After White's 1 P-KKt4, he threatens an attack on the position with 2 P-B5, but not with 2 P-Kt5!

*Diagram 36*

*Diagram 37*

From the position in diagram 37 White attacks with 1 P-Kt6. Now if 1 ... RP×P; 2 P×P, opening the Rook's file if 1 ... BP×P; 2 P-R6! forcing an opening of the Rook's file by sacrificing a pawn. Note that after 1 P-R6, Black could reply

1 ... P–Kt3 and, since the aim with a Rook would be the opening of a file and not a diagonal, this could no longer be achieved. Thus 1 P–R6 would be a mistake, and rob White's pawns of subsequent mobility.

Diagram 38 shows a similar position. This time, however, White wishes to open up the diagonal for the combined attack of his Queen and Bishop. Thus in this case not P–Kt6, but 1 P–R6! is the move required.

Diagram 38

Diagram 39

With the position as shown in diagram 39, 1 P–Kt5, although it drives away the Knight, would be a mistake. By moving 1 ... Kt–R4 the whole operation would be held up. But after 1 P–R5, White's pawns remain mobile, and may subsequently be able to open up a file for his Rook.

### The Pawns in Defence and as a Static Force

In contrast to their duties as a mobile force, the pawns are often required for functions of a more static nature, such as the occupation or control of an important square, or squares, or the formation of a barrier against infiltration of opposing pieces.

We already know that pawns are most effective in driving away pieces. It follows, therefore, that—

(1) Pawns are generally better for use in controlling or occupying important squares than pieces.

If a piece is used to occupy an important square, it can often be driven away by hostile pawns. Even distant control by a piece can often be nullified by an opposing pawn. In this connexion an important square might be one which could otherwise be used by opposing pawns to drive away your own pieces.

For instance, in the position in diagram 40, were the White pawns not at QR4 and Q5, the Knight could be driven away by the opposing Knight's pawn or Queen's pawn. Note here that if Black were to play 1 ... P–R3 as a preliminary to P–Kt4, attempting to drive the Knight away 2 P–R5, would nullify this and enable the Knight to move to QKt6 if required.

The correct procedure if Black wishes to try and dislodge the Knight would be to play 1 P–Kt3 (preventing P–R5), and follow with 2 P–R3, and then P–Kt4.

*Diagram 40*

(2) As a static unit, the pawns as a whole are strongest when they are in their original positions on the second rank.

Why is this so?

In the first place they are well away from the opponent's camp and in the heart of their own. They are thus well protected by the pieces behind them, and in addition present a "united-front" against attack from the opponent's pieces, which would have to advance far from their own base to make such an attack.

The reader knows, however, that the pawns have important *mobile* duties to perform during the course of the game, some of which can be done most efficiently only by pawns, and will not, therefore, be tempted by this knowledge to refrain from moving any of his pawns at all! Nevertheless, the observations first made show how important it is not to move pawns *unnecessarily* away from the second rank. (Remember advice about not moving pawns in front of the castled King.) Very often a pawn is needed for a static function well up the board, but then is more liable to be attacked than on the second rank.

(3) A pawn is best defended by another pawn.

When it is so defended a piece which takes it will be liable to capture from the defending pawn, thus involving loss of material in taking the pawn.

In diagram 41 the black pawn at Q4 is defended by another pawn. Now if 1 Kt×P, P×Kt; 2 B×P, White has lost a piece (worth three pawns) and gained only two pawns.

*Diagram 41*

If, however, the black Queen's Bishop's pawn were replaced by a Bishop, we would have 1 Kt×P, B×Kt; 2 B×B, and it is Black who has lost a clear pawn.

Thus, owing to its low relative value, a pawn defended by another pawn is generally safe from an attack by an opponent's piece, but not so if it is defended by pieces and subjected to attack from a superior force of opposing pieces.

The advantages of pawns in occupying and/or controlling important squares are therefore—

(1) They are not liable to be captured or driven away by pieces, if defended by another pawn.

(2) They can attack and drive off opposing pieces.

*Further Pawn Movements during the course of the Game*

During the course of the game, pawns are moved for various reasons.

For example—

*Dynamic Functions.* (1) In the course of a general advance or attack, or in capturing and "hand to hand" fighting in perhaps an attempt to open up a file or diagonal.

(2) To drive opposing pieces off important squares.

(3) To defend themselves when attacked.

*Static Functions.* (4) To occupy or control squares important to their own team or the opponent's.

(5) To defend another pawn which is being attacked.

### THE STRUCTURAL FACTOR IN PAWN FORMATIONS

First let us consider three pawns in their original formation on the board. This, of course, may occur further up the board than the second rank.

What are the outstanding features of such a pawn formation? (diagram 42).

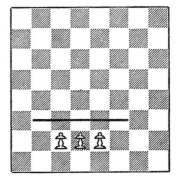

*Diagram 42*

In the first place the pawns exert pressure on five squares in a direct line in front of them, thus presenting the "united-front" against enemy attack, previously mentioned. No opposing piece could approach as far as these squares directly in front of them without risk of capture.

Similarly, there is no "hole" through which a piece could

infiltrate and perhaps attack them from the rear, or attack the pieces behind them. Such a formation is obviously very strong so long as it can be maintained.

Let us suppose that an outside pawn had to be played up one square for some reason. We would then have the formation depicted in diagram 43.

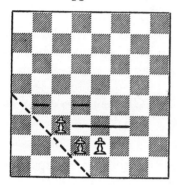

*Diagram 43*

At once, we notice that, although the pawns still control five squares in front of them, these five squares are no longer an unbroken line (the unbroken front has indeed been reduced to three squares). In addition the moving forward of that pawn has opened up a possible diagonal (as illustrated) for the infiltration of an opposing piece or pieces. The moving forward of one outside pawn has thus weakened the intrinsic strength of these three pawns.

Now in diagram 44 we see the formation resulting if both outside pawns have been moved up one square.

The "unbroken" front is no longer in existence, only three squares are controlled by the pawns and there is not one, but no less than four diagonals along which opposing pieces could infiltrate. Also one new weakness has been exposed. A weak square in the centre of the pawn formation. If an opponent's piece lodged in this square, it could *not* be driven off by the pawns, and in addition would hold back the rear

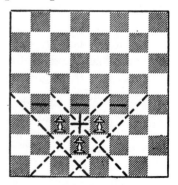

*Diagram 44*

pawn indefinitely. This formation, intrinsically, must be regarded as *very* weak.

The final possibility to consider for the moment is when the centre one of the three pawns has been advanced, as illustrated in diagram 45.

There are two "infiltration" diagonals, but the pawns are controlling four squares. This time the square in the centre of the formation is not as weak as in the previous example, since a piece there would not hold back the pawns, although the two squares in front of the outside pawns are weak squares.

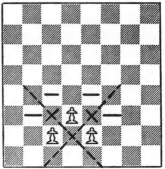

*Diagram 45*

We may conclude, therefore, that when in line abreast the pawns are in themselves strongest, less so when one of the outside ones has been advanced. They are weak if the centre pawn has been advanced, and considerably weaker if both the outside pawns have been advanced.

*Diagram 46*

The reader is again reminded of the care needed even when making a pawn-move!

### THE FUNCTIONAL FACTOR IN PAWN FORMATIONS

There is, however, another factor to be taken into consideration when analysing pawn formations. The one already discussed may be called their *structural* strength or weakness, but the other factor is their *functional* strength or weakness.

In other words, the work they are doing, and the position on the board they are occupying.

Suppose, referring to diagram 46, that Black's Q5 (White's Q4) were a square of vital importance to the course of the game.

Now, although the formation of the black pawns is, we know, structurally weak, nevertheless this disadvantage might be counterbalanced by the fact that it is exerting considerable pressure on the Q5, with two supported pawns bearing on that square. Consequently, on balance, the formation might be strong. But, if the black Q5 square were not of any special importance, then the black pawn formation might be weaker than the white one in this diagram.

The weak square they cause is situated in the centre of the board. If White has, say, castled QR, it might not be nearly so beneficial for Black to occupy Kt6, as it would be for White to occupy the central Q5 (Black's Q4). So, in addition, there is another consideration and that is, *that a weakness of structure is less important if in a less important position.* A wing position may, of course, be a very important one as, for instance, in front of a castled King.

Diagram 47

In diagram 47 we have an illustration of another possible formation of three pawns not yet discussed.

The white pawns are strong by virtue of the fact that the front two are each defended by another pawn, and that they are occupying and controlling important central squares.

They must, therefore, be stronger in these respects than the black pawns shown here, since the structure is the same but they are better situated.

Let us examine this formation as we did the previous ones.

In diagram 48 we see a position, similar to the previous one, illustrating the intrinsic weakness of this formation. Note the weak square in front of the rear one of the three pawns.

On the other hand if those squares are controlled by a piece of the same colour, the net result of such formation may indeed be an

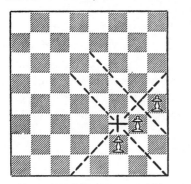
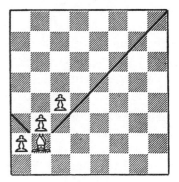

Diagram 48                    Diagram 49

advantage. In diagram 49 the Bishop has a clear diagonal for his control, and "defends" the weak square in front of the rear pawn.

Further aspects of this pawn formation are discussed on pages 53–7.

SUMMARY

Now let us summarize what has been achieved in first discussing the pawns in general.

Two main activities of the pawns have been shown—they can have dynamic "attacking" duties, and static "defensive" type of duties. We have established standards by which the usefulness of a pawn or pawns can be judged.

(1) The Structural Factor. Are the pawns strong inherently—by virtue of their formation?

(2) The Functional Factor. Are they performing a useful function?

When making pawn moves always consider these closely complementary factors. In order to perform a certain function it is essential that the pawn, or pawns be inherently strong enough for the task, otherwise they will be lost. In addition, the stronger they are structurally the more ambitious may be the task which they can successfully accomplish!

## PAWN WEAKNESSES

The main pawn weaknesses which so often occur during the game are enumerated below. Great difficulty was experienced by the authors in finding definitions which accurately and fully describe these various pawn manifestations, but it is vitally important for the reader to understand each one thoroughly. Unless you see why a pawn cannot be, say, isolated unless it complies with the definitions given below, you may be tempted to concentrate on an "imaginary" weakness in the opponent's position, and find it suddenly turned into a tower of strength!

### ISOLATED PAWNS

A pawn is isolated so long as it remains incapable of receiving immediate support from, or of giving immediate support to, another pawn. ("Immediate" here means "in one move".)

Diagram 50

*Example.* In diagram 50 the white Queen's Rook's pawn is a simple isolated pawn.

The white Queen's pawn is also an isolated pawn, as owing to the black King's pawn it cannot receive immediate support from another pawn. In addition, the white King's pawn is also isolated.

It should be noted that the black King's pawn is not isolated, since it can receive support from the King's Bishop's pawn immediately if necessary. Another interesting point is, of course, that neither the white King's pawn nor Queen's pawn need always be isolated since, if the black King's pawn were subsequently captured, the uniting of these two pawns would become possible once more.

Now, what are the points, both for and against an isolated pawn? How does it stand up to our pawn judgment?

*Weaknesses*

Its primary weakness is that it cannot be supported by another pawn (so long as it remains isolated). We know that it thus lacks its *best* means of support, and is subject to attack from opposing pieces.

Another weakness must be the *square* immediately in front of it. Since it has no pawn support, an opposing piece taking up position on this square cannot be driven off by pawns and would thus be difficult to dislodge. While remaining there, the piece would hold up any advance of the isolated pawn. So an isolated pawn, especially when well advanced, is going to be very difficult to defend and may even be lost—and the game with it!

*Exploiting the Weaknesses of an Isolated Pawn*

Maxim: *First blockade, then attack!*

It is most important to prevent the isolated pawn from moving forward. It then becomes a sitting target to be attacked, always much easier than one in flight and, in addition, blocking prevents any attempt to exchange it, perhaps with an unisolated pawn of your own. Having blockaded it, then attack it, though it may be necessary or expedient to delay this attack until quite late in the game.

A typically good disposition of forces against an isolated pawn is shown in diagram 51. Here we have the Knight at Q4 doing the actual blockading of the isolated pawn. (Note that this

Knight cannot be driven away by any hostile pawn.) The other
Knight and the Bishop have it "under fire." The Rook is placed

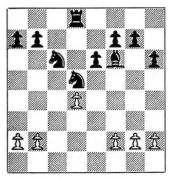

on that file so that, if and when
the Knight moves, the pawn
will be menaced by no less
than three pieces. In consequence White will need at least
three pieces to prevent loss of
the pawn in this event, and these
pieces will be tied down to
the defence of a pawn, whereas
all Black's pieces can, if required, be used or diverted for
other purposes.

*Diagram 51*

In diagram 52 the white Queen's pawn is again isolated. Black
plays 1 ... Kt–KB4; and in spite of his equality in pieces White
is unable to prevent the pawn being captured. Note that the
isolated pawn is blockaded by the black pawn and then attacked.

*Diagram 52*                    *Diagram 53*

Another typical manœuvre for winning an isolated pawn is
illustrated in diagram 53. In this instance the isolated pawn under
discussion is Black's Queen's Bishop's pawn. This is on a

semi-open file (see page 57) and against the threatened 1 P-Q6, Black cannot avoid the loss of this pawn.

If 1 . . . R-Q2; 2 . . . R-B6, followed by P-Q6.

*Compensations for an Isolated Pawn*

If the reader has acquired an isolated pawn, our advice is "despair not," there are a number of compensations which generally occur in connexion with an isolated pawn. There can be—

(1) An open file or files.

(2) Greater mobility for your pieces.

(3) Latent power of mobility of the pawn,

if your opponent fails to blockade it.

### (1) and (2)

In diagram 54 the first two of these factors are illustrated. White has an isolated Queen's pawn, but as a result he has an open file with great mobility for his Rook, and his Queen has also a greater range of activity, than would be possible if a pawn were on QB3 or K3 defending the Queen's pawn.

Make use, therefore, of any open files or greater space for manœuvring afforded if you are "saddled" with an isolated pawn.

*Diagram 54*

### (3)

In the appended diagram, Black has not blockaded White's isolated pawn. The result is that White has manœuvred into a position where 1 P-Q5, would win a piece, opening up the Bishop's diagonal and threatening mate, at the same time attacking the black Knight.

*Diagram 55*

Properly exploited, an isolated pawn must generally be a weakness, since it cannot be supported by another pawn, but full use should be made of any compensatory advantages in the event of having one of your own pawns isolated.

On occasions the *functional* value of an isolated pawn may outweigh the structural weakness of its isolation.

### DOUBLED PAWNS

Two pawns of the same colour on the same file are known as Doubled Pawns. In its simplest form, this definition requires no explanation, that is when the doubled pawns are also both isolated pawns.

In this case, of course, they have all the disadvantages and compensations of a simple isolated pawn, with the difference that if one is directly behind the other, then the blockading of the front one, leads to the blockading of two pawns.

The exploitation of the weakness is the same as for a single isolated pawn—first blockade, then attack.

A formation of three pawns, however, two of which are doubled, must be examined more closely in order to discover the weaknesses and other factors connected with it.

In diagram 56 we have a formation of three pawns, two of which are doubled. Examining this formation in a way similar to that in which the pawn formations were examined on pages 33–44, what do we find? First, there is an unbroken front across the board of four squares on which the two front pawns are exerting pressure. In addition, one of the front pawns is receiving support from the rear of the doubled pawns.

Compared, however, with the formation where all three pawns are abreast, it has the disadvantage of less "consecutive" square control, and no means of support for the rear pawn which

*Diagram 56*

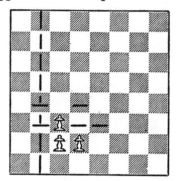

*Diagram 57*

cannot move forward. The file marked in the diagram affords some compensation, as it can usually be controlled by the player with the doubled pawns.

This next formation (diagram 57) has reasonable square control though of an irregular and broken type. However, it is clearly not especially weak, particularly as it can usually be transposed into the first mentioned formation.

At once we can notice the weakness of this third structure (diagram 58). Any semblance of an unbroken front is gone—two diagonals in addition to the file have been opened up for infiltration by opposing pieces, and a very weak square appears in front of the doubled pawns. It can be seen that in this position neither of the doubled pawns can be protected, except by pieces.

The final possibility with this type of pawn formation is shown in diagram 59. Although the front pawns are strong in themselves, being each protected by another pawn, the formation is "full of holes." Two diagonals are opened up for possible use by the opponent, and the square marked in the centre of the formation is weak because an opposing piece lodged there could not be dislodged, except by other pieces. In the position shown, Black's pawn and Bishop render the whole formation immobile.

What conclusion can be reached then, concerning these "complex" doubled pawns?

First, they are all weaker than their corresponding types of formations when there are no pawns doubled, since in reality the

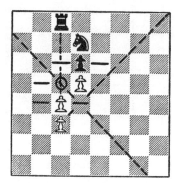

Diagram 58                    Diagram 59

rear one of the doubled pawns merely assists to a greater or less degree the activities of the other two and does not itself play an active part in the formation. In addition the rear pawn is weak as it cannot receive support from another pawn. Structurally the best formation is to have two pawns in line abreast in front, with the other doubled pawn in the rear, as in the first diagram.

The second formation is also quite strong, but the other two formations are clearly weaker. As far as liability to attack is concerned, the third is the weakest. The functional factor has, of course, also to be considered in these as in all pawn formations.

## BACKWARD PAWNS

A pawn is considered backward when it is unsupported by another pawn, is incapable of receiving immediate support from another pawn, and is unable itself to move forward out of its backwardness without material loss or positional disadvantage accruing from such movement.

This seemingly complicated definition will be understood readily when we apply it, as in diagram 60.

Now in this diagram, Black's Queen's pawn is a backward pawn. It is not capable of receiving support from another pawn in one move, and although it can itself move forward, it cannot do so without Black's losing a pawn—in this case, the backward pawn itself. Note that it is not an isolated pawn since it is clearly united with the black King's pawn.

One interesting point is that a backward pawn is *already blockaded*, since it cannot move forward without loss, but in the position in the diagram the

*Diagram 60*

square in front of it is a weak square, so the posting of a piece there is likely to be an advantage to White, even apart from making quite sure that the backward pawn is unable to move. Note also that if the black Queen's pawn were on Q2, it would still be a backward pawn for although it could move forward to Q3 without loss, it would not have moved forward *out of its backwardness*, since we know it is still backward at Q3.

In diagram 61 we have another illustration of an attack on a backward pawn. Note that it immobilizes the black Rook in its defence, whilst White's Rook has the whole file on which to manœuvre and still maintain the pressure.

The weaknesses of a backward pawn, therefore, may be summarized as follows—

(1) It can only be protected by pieces when attacked, as in the case of an isolated pawn.

(2) Usually the square in front of a backward pawn is a *weak square*, a minor positional strongpoint for the opponent.

(3) A pawn majority containing a backward pawn might be immobilized by a minority of opposing pawns.

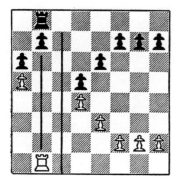

Diagram 61                    Diagram 62

For instance, examine the position in diagram 62. Though Black has one more pawn in this position. White, by playing P–Kt5, could render both the black Rook's pawn and Bishop's pawn backward and thus all three wing pawns would be held up by one white pawn. Note here that this shows another weakness of the three-pawn formation mentioned on pages 39–43, where Black's centre pawn has been played up one square.

In dealing with a backward plan the principle is the same as for the isolated pawns. We might say in this case, "First ensure that the blockade cannot be lifted, then attack!"

In the course of a game, having a pawn that cannot be moved forward is very likely to burden its possessor with a cramped game. Pawns as we know are moved forward to release pieces, among other reasons. Being unable to move a pawn forward is, therefore, liable to mean that pieces may not become fully mobile, with a cramped game resulting.

### The Effect of a Pawn Blocking a Pawn-weakness

If an opponent's pawn, rather than a piece, occupies the weak square in front of a pawn weakness, it very often has the effect of reducing the weakness by reducing the avenues of attack against it.

A previous diagram is reproduced but with a black pawn on B4 (diagram 63). Clearly this pawn blocks the Rook's attack and takes away an excellent square for the Knight. Note, however, that it does not prevent a Black attack by Kt–K4. Where possible, the weak square in front of an inferior pawn formation should be occupied by a piece rather than a pawn.

*Diagram 63*

## THE PAWN-CHAIN

A formation of pawns is known as a pawn-chain when each pawn in the formation gives support to the one in front. Generally it is a diagonal line of pawns supporting one another.

As mentioned under "General Considerations," the individual pawns in a pawn-chain are strong, since each pawn except the rear one is supported by another pawn. In addition, if the pawn-chain is situated in the centre of the board, it is liable to have a very cramping effect on the opponent, rather after the style of a series of pill boxes in warfare.

The inherent strength of a pawn-chain makes it compare favourably even with the "line abreast" pawn formation. To effect a break-through in the centre for instance, it may be necessary to try to "destroy" an opposing pawn-chain. How can this be achieved?

There are three possibilities. We have seen that all the pawns are supported except the pawn at the base of the chain. The first possibility to consider must therefore, be—

(1) Attack at its base.

Since the base pawn must be defended by pieces, that may well be its weakest link, as for instance in the position shown in diagram 64.

However, while it may be most desirable to attack a pawn-chain at its base, that may not be always possible or practicable, particularly for instance if the base pawn stands on the second rank.

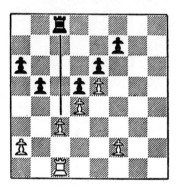

Diagram 64

The next possibility, therefore, is—

(2) Attack against the centre of the chain.

The advantage of attacking at its centre is that if the particular pawn attacked makes a capture, the pawn-chain is immediately cut in two!

In diagram 65, for instance, we have a position in which the white pawn-chain is being attacked at its centre by the black pawn at QB4. If White does take pawn with pawn, not only has the white pawn-chain been exploded, but for the gain of a pawn he will be saddled with doubled isolated pawns, both of which may well be lost later in the game.

If White, however, does not take the pawn, then Black may elect to do so next move.

Diagram 66 shows a likely result after Black has taken pawn

with pawn. Looking first at the pawns, we note that the white pawn-chain has been reduced from three to two pawns, and that the "weak" base pawn has moved up nearer the opponent and is thus more liable to attack. In fact, it has become a backward pawn, already blockaded, and since Black has attacked it with

Diagram 65

Diagram 66

two pieces, White has been compelled to "immobilize" two pieces in its defence.

Neither of these methods may be possible however, so that it may be necessary to adopt what is generally the least advantageous method.

(3) Attack the first pawn in the chain.

In this position (diagram 67) Black has attacked the first pawn in the chain with 1 ... P–B3. If White takes 2 P×P, then 2 ... P×P and the white pawn-chain is reduced to two pawns, with the further possibility of Black's making a second attack against the front one of these two by 3 ... P–K4. If 4 P×P, P×P and White has now an isolated pawn and no chain!

If, however, White declines to take the pawn in the first place, Black may do so next move, e.g. 2 ... P×P. Now, if White retakes with a pawn (3 P×P) he has two isolated pawns and no chain. If capturing with a Knight, then the same position arises after Black's Kt × Kt, White having at least one isolated pawn. Note that this attack against the leading pawn of the chain would

*Diagram 67*

yield no advantage if White's King's Bishop's pawn were not blocked by his Knight. White could then reply to 1 ... P–B3; with 2 P–KB4, and maintain the pawn-chain intact.

As capturing an attacking pawn is not liable to benefit the pawn-chain as a whole, it is often possible to make two attacks against it before pressing home either.

In the next diagram, we have a position exemplifying this.

At the moment White has a four-pawn chain (diagram 68). Black has attacked this pawn-chain both in its centre by P–QB4

and at the leading pawn by P–KB3. Very often one sees Black playing P–B5 in similar positions to this. Why may this be wrong? The reader will see that this move immediately relieves White's sorely harassed pawn-chain. From being subjected to a double attack on it, he has now only to face the easiest attack to deal with— that against the leading pawn.

*Diagram 68*

It may not necessarily be best to explode the chain *immediately*. It may be better from Black's point of view if the tension is maintained, since he is the attacker, and White the defender.

An attack on a pawn-chain may occur quite early in a game, as in the example on the opposite page.

| | | |
|---|---|---|
| 1 | P–K4 | P–K3 |
| 2 | P–Q4 | P–Q4 |
| 3 | Kt–QB3 | Kt–KB3 |
| 4 | B–Kt5 | B–K2 |
| 5 | P–K5 | KKt–Q2 |
| 6 | B × B | Q × B |
| 7 | Q–Q2 | O–O |
| 8 | Kt–Q1 | |

Anticipating Black's attack on the base on his two-pawn chain

| | | |
|---|---|---|
| 8 | ... | P–QB4 |
| 9 | P–QB3 | Kt–QB3 |
| 10 | Kt–B3 | P–B3 |

White's pawn-chain is now attacked at its centre and at the first pawn in the chain.

*When moving a pawn watch the squares you lose as well as the squares you gain.*

### OPEN FILES AND THE SEVENTH RANK

#### OPEN FILES

Strictly speaking there are two types of open files—

(*a*) *Absolute Open Files*. These are files entirely devoid of pawns.

(*b*) *Semi-open Files*. These are files devoid of pawns of one colour. In diagram 69, for example, White has control of an absolute open file, on the Queen's side and a semi-open file on the King's side.

What are the uses and advantages of open files? Let us return to our comparison of chess with warfare.

An absolute open file can be considered as an unblocked pass between mountains. Whichever side controls that pass can manœuvre or deploy his forces along and through it, and penetrate into the enemy's position.

In the case of a semi-open file, the pass is still there, but one end is blocked. Nevertheless, if the enemy's end is blocked, it

may still be advisable to pour troops into the pass from the unblocked end, and an attempt be made to break through. If this is not achieved, enemy defenders will be immobilized there at the mouth of the pass, whereas the whole of the pass except the blocked end is available to your forces for manœuvring.

*Diagram 69*

Pressure on open and semi-open files is best achieved by placing a Rook on that file, and perhaps later obtaining more pressure by doubling the Rooks and even adding to this pressure with the Queen.

### Control of Absolute Open Files

Try to seize control of an open file. The player in control is likely to have more space for manœuvring his forces, and gain control of a greater area of the board. As we know, mobile pieces are more valuable than immobile ones.

*Diagram 70*

The importance of being *first* in placing one's Rook on an absolute open file, may be considerable, as there are generally pawns on at least one of the adjacent files.

In the position shown in diagram 70, the Queen's Bishop's file is open. Let us suppose White has the move. With 1 QR–B1,

he seizes the open file. Now Black can challenge this control by
1 ... QR–B1. But because White is there first he can reply
2 R–B5! Now if 2 ... R×R; 3 QP×R, and White has a
passed pawn.

(The passed pawn is described in detail in the section on the
End-game.) If Black does not take the Rook, White can double
his Rooks and keep control of the file. As the position is symmetrical, had Black had the move, his would be a similar
advantage.

The final benefit of control of an open file, is that it may
enable you to infiltrate into the enemy's position, and also to
occupy the SEVENTH RANK, the advantages of which are
discussed later in this chapter.

### Control of Semi-open Files

Though putting pressure on a semi-open file is sure to cause
discomfort to your opponent, the greatest benefit to the attacking
side is found when the blocking
piece is itself weak. The pressure
thus exerted on that weakness
may result in the capture of the
blockader and the full opening
of the file, or at least will tie
opposing pieces down to its
defence.

Diagram 71

In diagram 71 White is
exerting pressure on the semi-
open Queen's file. The blocking
pawn is a backward pawn, and
blockaded very effectively by the Rook which is utilizing to the
full the advantage of the "full length of the pass."

Now, having been blockaded, the backward pawn is attacked
by 1 Kt–K4. This compels 1 ... B–K2, or KR–Q1, and additional pressure by White's 2 Q–Q3, compels Black to play

whichever of those moves was not originally played. Note here how cramped and immobile are Black's pieces, a situation which in itself is not very healthy! In this particular position the backward pawn can be won by 3 P–B5 (if 3 ... KtP×P; 4 Kt×P, winning a Rook for the Knight).

These types of manœuvres are very common when exploiting semi-open files.

Open files generally occur in positions where there is tension, where there are pawns in a taking position, generally in the centre.

## THE SEVENTH RANK

The seventh rank is a minor positional strongpoint, and its occupation by a Rook or Queen, or combinations of both, gives distinct advantages to the occupier. The most important of these are enumerated below.

(1) He attacks the Opponent's pieces on that rank.

These are normally very difficult to defend, and in the case of pawns, since that rank is their base, they necessarily cannot be defended by other pawns, and so pieces must be utilized to defend them.

(2) It has a cramping effect on the opponent's pieces.

Since the pawns must be defended by pieces, these pieces tend to become immobilized as in the position in diagram 72. On the Queen's side both the Queen's Bishop's pawn and the black Rook are immobilized, if Black is to prevent loss of material. On the King's side if the Knight's pawn moves forward, then the Rook's pawn is attacked.

(3) It facilitates a direct attack on the King.

In the "skeleton" position in diagram 73, for instance, White has played the Rook from K4 to K7 threatening mate, and after

1 ... P–Kt3; 2 Q–R6, mate is inevitable. But had White played from K4 to KKt4 instead, though this still threatens mate, Black has three defences P–Kt3, R–R2 or R–B2.

(4) It frequently limits the opposing King to his first rank.

This is particularly an advantage in the end-game, when the

Diagram 72                         Diagram 73

Kings are so often needed in the centre of the board. (See End-game.) Any, or all of these advantages may occur in one and the same excursion to the seventh rank. Many examples of the usages and benefits occurring from these manœuvres will be found in the illustrative games in Chapter IV.

*Advice Concerning Open Files and the Seventh Rank*

(a) Seize the open file.

(b) Aim to establish a Rook on the seventh rank in the case of an absolute open file.

(c) If your opponent already controls an open file, try to oppose him on it (e.g. oppose Rook to Rook), and do not allow him to consolidate his hold.

(d) If there are two or more open files, and your opponent controls one, it may be preferable to try to gain control of another one rather than oppose him on the one he controls.

## THE KNIGHT OUTPOST

The Knight, as a chess piece, is unique. All the other pieces have at least some factors in common with one another, but none in common with the Knight.

The Knight possesses the following characteristics not shared by any other piece—

(1) Its *mode* of movement.

(2) Its power to *jump over* other pieces.

These peculiarities in turn lead to the following—

(1) When it attacks a dissimilar piece, that piece cannot be attacking it.

(2) No defending piece can be interposed against attack from a Knight—to avoid capture the attacked piece must move, or else the Knight be captured by another piece. (In the case of a Knight checking, the King must move or the Knight be taken immediately.)

These unique powers of the Knight exercise their maximum effect on an opponent when that Knight can occupy an OUT-POST—either in the centre or the opponent's half of the board.

A KNIGHT OUTPOST is a square which a Knight can occupy, either in the centre or enemy-half of the board, and from which it cannot be driven without material loss or positional disadvantage to the opponent.

An ideal outpost is generally a central square on the opponent's *third rank*.

*Example—*

The white Knight in diagram 74 is occupying an outpost. Note that the black Bishop operates on white squares and cannot thus be exchanged for the Knight.

Note also that Black cannot dislodge the Knight's support by P–B3 as the supporting pawn is defended by the Queen's pawn.

A similar, but perhaps slightly more common type of Knight outpost is shown in diagram 75.

Here Black is in a position to jump into Q5 with the Knight

Diagram 74

Diagram 75

which will then block the backward pawn and be extremely difficult to dislodge.

What, then, are the main advantages of obtaining a Knight Outpost?

(1) It has a cramping effect on the opponent.

Examine again diagram 74. In this position the Knight cannot be dislodged except at the cost of a Rook. While it remains there, however, Black's pieces are very difficult to manœuvre. His Bishop cannot develop without risk of losing the QKtP, while the Rooks have between them but three squares on to which they can move without being captured. Remember that the Knight can exert pressure on *eight* different squares at the same time.

In diagram 75 the mere possibility of the Knight occupying the Q5 square leaves White with a very limited choice of movement.

*Diagram 76*

(2) It frequently induces pawn weaknesses in an opponent's position.

The two positions shown in diagram 76 represent a common type of "pseudo" outpost.

By occupying these, White leaves his opponent with two alternatives. Either he does nothing, in which case the squares become true outposts for the Knights, or else he drives them away and thus weakens his pawn formations.

### Restraint in Occupying Outposts

Diagram 77 shows a position similar to the second. Here Black has a potential outpost at his Q5, but he would be un-wise to occupy it immediately since after Kt × Kt, White has good chances of advancing with P–QKt4 (if QBP × Kt) or P–KB4 (if KP × Kt), whereas Black will have blocked White's backward Queen's pawn with a pawn. (Remember the end of the section "Pawn Weaknesses.")

Do not as a rule actually occupy an outpost until you can

*Diagram 77*

remain there for some time undisturbed, but always be on the look-out for possible Knight outposts. Many famous players have considered a Knight which is firmly entrenched on an out-post, to be at least the equal of a Rook.

## PINNING AND DISCOVERIES

The manœuvres in chess known as "Pinning" and "Discoveries" are closely related. Before the more important pinning can be fully understood, it is necessary to deal first with the discovery. What is a discovery?

DISCOVERIES

A discovery is made when—

(*a*) The movement of a piece causes a check on the opponent's King *by a piece other than the piece moved.*

(*b*) The movement of a piece leads to the exposure of an opponent's piece to attack from a piece other than the one moved.

In either of these cases, the discovery may be a *double* threat, which occurs *when the piece moved, as well as the other piece,* takes part in the checking or attack. Let us consider some examples of discoveries.

In diagram 78 the black King is not in check, but by moving the Bishop away White can expose the King to check from his Rook.

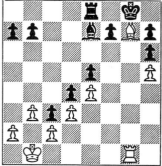

From the point of view of the defender in such positions, the discovery should usually be treated *as if the King were already in check*, since a discovered check can be a very powerful threat.

*Diagram 78*

For instance, with White to move in this position he wins the game by utilizing this power of discovery in the following manner—

| 1 | B × RP *dis. ch* | K–R1 |
| 2 | B–Kt7 *ch* | K–Kt1 |
| 3 | B × P *ch* | K–B1 |

| 4 | B–Kt7 *ch* | K–Kt1 |
|---|------------|-------|
| 5 | B × P *ch* | K–B1  |
| 6 | B–Kt7 *ch* | K–Kt1 |
| 7 | B × P *ch* | K–B1  |
| 8 | B–Kt7 *ch* | K–Kt1 |
| 9 | B–Q4 *ch*  | K–B1  |
| 10 | B × QRP   |       |

(all Black's moves are forced)
and White should win with his three pawn advantage.

If it were Black's move, however, by considering his King already in check and playing.

| 1 | ... | B–Kt4 |
|---|-----|-------|

then after

| 2 | B × RP  | P–B3  |
|---|---------|-------|
| 3 | B × B   | P × B |
| 4 | R × P *ch* | K–B2 |

White has only even material. This illustrates definition (*a*).

*Diagram 79*

We have already mentioned that a discovery may constitute a double threat, or DOUBLE CHECK. Examine the position in diagram 79.

Black by 1 . . ., Kt–Q5 threatens to win a Rook, as mate is threatened by the discovery (if 2 R × R, R × R and the mate threat remains). But with White's reply he has a DOUBLE CHECK! 2 B–K6 dbl ch!!

*In the case of a double check the King must always move*, since two pieces cannot be captured or defended against in one move. In this position the King must move to Kt1, after which we have R–B8 *mate*.

In diagram 80 we have an example of the other type of discovery (definition (*b*) above).

In this position Black is to play. He appears to be able to win a pawn by 1 ... P×P; 2 P×P, Kt×P; 3 Kt×Kt, Q×Kt. But

*Diagram* 80

*Diagram* 81

should he attempt this, then White replies 4 B–Kt5 *ch*, exposing the black Queen to attack. Since the move is a double threat, the Queen is in fact lost.

When there is a choice between an actual check, and a move in which your opponent may be subjected to a discovered check afterwards, it is often preferable to use the threat rather than the actual check.

For instance, in diagram 81 White has to capture the black Knight on B2 to equalize in material.

Now, after 1 B×Kt *ch*, K–R1 and White has no advantage. But after 1 R×Kt, he attacks the Queen and also threatens a discovered check. In this case no matter where the Queen flees to she is lost. Thus for example 1 R×Kt, Q–Q1; 2 R–Q7 *dis. ch* wins the Queen.

## PINNING

Now a pin is closely associated with a discovery. If we were to replace the pieces performing the discoveries, in all the previous examples, with similar pieces of the *opposite* colour, those pieces would be considered PINNED, because they then could not be moved without, say, exposing the King to check, or other pieces to attack.

*Definition.* A piece is considered pinned—

(*a*) When it is unable to move owing to a check being discovered.

(*b*) When moving it would expose a piece of high value to attack from an opposing piece of lower value.

(*c*) When moving it would threaten mate or loss of material to one's own side.

*Note.* It is only in the case of definition (*a*) that the pinned piece is unable to move. Under the other definitions, it can sometimes be moved if, for instance, the threat thus created is so great that the loss of the piece behind it does not matter.

*Example—Definition* (*a*)

In diagram 82 the black Rook is pinned, since it cannot move without exposing the King to check. A "pin on the diagonal."

| *Diagram* 82 | *Diagram* 83 |

The Knight is also pinned, on the file.

*Example—Definition* (*b*)

In diagram 83 the Knight is pinned, since to move it would expose the Queen to attack from the Bishop. Its capture is threatened by P–K5.

*Example—Definition* (*c*)

A piece is considered pinned when moving it would threaten mate or loss of material to one's own side.

In diagram 84 the black Knight is pinned on the file, since the Rook would be lost if he moved. However, it should be noted that, if the black Knight were on R3 instead of R2, it would not

Diagram 84                          Diagram 85

be pinned, since then it would move to KB2 thus defending the Rook. 1 Kt–Kt5, is threatened.

In diagram 85, White is able to play 1 Q×Kt, because the pawn is pinned by the Bishop and after this move the black Bishop is securely pinned and mate must follow.

Again, in the position shown in diagram 86, the white Bishop is pinned because of the R–Kt8 *mate* threat. After Black plays 1 ... B–KR6 White cannot avoid mate by Rook or Bishop.

The next diagram (87) illustrates a somewhat more complicated position. Black has the move. Because of the numerous pins to which he can be subjected, White can be mated by the sacrificial 1 ... Q×Kt *ch*. Since the Bishop is pinned by the black Rook, 2 K×Q is forced. Then after 2 ... Kt–K6 *ch* the pawn cannot take; as it has become the subject of a pin from the other black Rook 3 K–Kt1 is, therefore, forced. We then have 3 ... R×B *ch* and White's moves are all forced. 4 K–R1, R–Kt8 *ch*; 5 K×R, R–Kt1 *ch*; 6 K–R1, B–B6 *mate*.

Diagram 86

Diagram 87

A pin is, generally speaking, more important than a discovery because it is of more frequent occurrence in games, and its main effects are often hidden, whereas a discovery which is pending is generally obvious to all but the most unobservant players!

### The Value of Pinning

The value of pinning an opposing piece or pieces is apt to be overlooked, or more properly we should say apt to be "taken for granted." The usual move of B–Kt5 pinning the opposing Knight is often done as a haphazard developing move, without full realization of its value or of the fact that it is not only an end in itself, but should be followed up if possible.

The value of pinning may be summarized thus—

(1) It immobilizes the pinned piece, and may also immobilize the piece which movement of the pinned piece would expose.

That alone may justify a pin since we know from our value of the pieces that an immobile piece is of less value than a mobile one.

(2) A pinned piece can be made the object of attack or pressure, and such attack or pressure may lead to loss of material, and/or other weaknesses, for example, isolated or doubled pawns.

### Value of Pressure on Pinned Pieces

A number of the advantages which may result from pressure on pinned pieces are illustrated below.

Examine the position shown in diagram 88.

It will be observed that the white Queen's Knight is pinned, but at the moment adequately defended. However, if it is Black's move, he can play 1 ... R–B1. He thus brings another piece to bear on the pinned Knight. This cannot be moved,

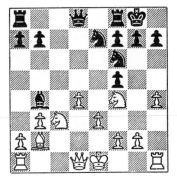

Diagram 88

so White must defend it, thus "immobilizing" another of his pieces. 2 R–QB1, this Rook is now "tied down" to the defence of the Knight 2 ... Q–R4. Once more the poor Queen's Knight needs protection. 3 Q–Q3, Kt–K5; 4 Kt–K2, Kt–Q4 and the Knight must fall.

So it can be seen that even if the piece were not to fall, one of the advantages of bringing pressure to bear on a pinned piece is that many opposing pieces may be immobilized in defence of it.

Now study diagram 89. Black to move. With 1 ... R–K1 *ch* Black can force a pin! If White replies with 2 Kt–K5, then 2 ... P–B3 would win the Knight, so he must play 2 B–K2, B–R3; pressure is brought to bear on the pinned piece.

3 Kt–Kt1. Poor Knight, he looks doomed to obscurity in the house where he was born! 3 ... R×B *ch*. Why the sacrifice? At present Black cannot win the pinned piece, but by this sacrifice he is able to maintain the pin and reduce the defenders by one.

*Diagram 89*

4 Kt×R. The gallant Knight decides not to die in bed at home, but to perish on the fields of battle! 4 ... R—K1, and White has nothing left to defend the Knight with, except by sacrificing his Queen.

If 5 O–O we get 5 ... B×Kt winning back the Rook and remaining a piece up. If he moves the Queen, we have 5 ... R×Kt *ch*; 6 K–B1 and now he is in a very unpleasant discovery. If he doesn't move the King or Queen, 5 ... R×Kt *ch* wins it. By forcing the pin, bringing pressure to bear on it, and persevering with that pin even to the extent of a sacrifice, Black has achieved a great advantage in what otherwise might have been a fairly even position.

### The Pin in Indirect Attack and Defence

The PIN may also be used as a means of an indirect attack or defence.

In diagram 90 the white King's pawn is threatened because

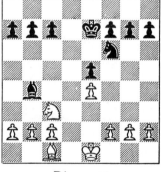

*Diagram 90*

the Knight defending it is pinned. If White now plays B–Kt5, the attacking Knight is pinned, and the pawn is, therefore, defended adequately.

### The Hidden Element in Pins

We mentioned previously that one of the reasons why pinning requires more attention is that its presence or effects can more readily be hidden than those of a discovery. The reader should

*Diagram 91*

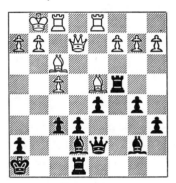

*Diagram 92*

be very careful in searching for hidden pins, some of which, when coupled with latent discoveries, are very powerful weapons.

Such a position is illustrated in diagram 91, it being closely interwoven with a discovery. The hidden pin/discovery is exploited after White's 1 P×P. Then if 1 ... KP×P, 2 Kt×P and the pinned Queen's Bishop's pawn cannot retake without loss of the Queen. If 1 ... BP×P, then again, 2 Kt×P and the discovery on the Queen precludes capture of the Knight.

Finally, there is the pin which is hidden because a sacrifice has to be used to bring it about (diagram 92).

*Diagram 93*

Black plays 1 ... R×B! Why? Because realizing the power

and value of a pin, he sees 2 R×R, B–B4 and the Rook thus pinned is lost; since however it is defended, say 3 P–B3, P–K4 will win it.

Another example of taking advantage of a pin is shown in diagram 93.

Black has just played 1 ... B–B3 in an effort to exchange off White's well placed Bishop. White, however, observing that the Knight is pinned owing to the unprotected Bishop, exploits that pin by 2 B–Q5! If 2 ... B×B; 3 P×B winning a piece. If 2 ... B–Q2; 3 Q–K2 and Black must still lose a piece.

### The Use of Pins in Producing Other Weaknesses

As already mentioned, pins may be used to produce those other types of weaknesses and strategic concepts already mentioned. In other words, though pressure on a pin may produce

Diagram 94

good results "in itself," it may be that the conversion of a pin into another type of weakness, may be the way to a victory. The reader must remember that all these weaknesses and strategic concepts are not in little water-tight compartments of their own. They are all parts, and indeed interchangeable parts, of the game of chess as a whole. They often dovetail one into

the other, and a pin perhaps cannot advantageously be maintained, but may instead be converted into bringing about, say, a pawn weakness, in the opponent's position, as for instance in diagram 94.

Here, White can, because of the discovered pin on the Bishop when his Knight moves, play 1 Kt×Kt and Black is forced to recapture with the pawn, which then becomes an *isolated pawn*.

Again in the fairly common type of opening position shown in diagram 95, White can bring pressure to bear on the pinned Knight by 1 Kt-Q5. Whatever other advantages White may be able to gain by this pressure, Black is compelled to submit at the least to a *doubled pawn*.

In diagram 96 the black Queen's pawn is pinned, since after

Diagram 95

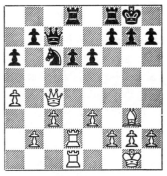

Diagram 96

1 ... P-Q4; 2 B×Q, P×Q; 3 B×R he loses the exchange. The only means of defending it is therefore 1 ... P-K4; and now the weakness of the Queen's pawn is no longer that it is pinned, but that it has become a *backward pawn!*

It will be seen, therefore, that pinning is a very important strategic concept. It is not only an end in itself (the immobilization of one or more opposing pieces), but it can be the means of producing other weaknesses.

*Advice Concerning Pinning*

(a) Inflict a pin, as a general rule, whenever possible.

(b) Try to put pressure on the pinned piece.

(c) When you are pinned, try to get out of the pin as soon as you can, and before pressure can be brought to bear on your pinned piece.

(*d*) Beware of potential or "hidden" pins.

A familiarity with all types of actual and hidden pins, and a knowledge of how to take advantage of them is a strong weapon in the hands of its possessor, and the placing of a piece in a position in which it inflicts a pin, is, indeed, "the occupation of a minor positional strongpoint!"

## THE ART OF EXCHANGING

What is an exchange? In chess it consists of giving up one of your pieces in order to capture a piece of equal, greater, or less value belonging to your opponent. An exchange, however, will frequently *alter the positional considerations* as well, and it is with this factor that we are chiefly concerned, since to capture, say, an opponent's Queen at the expense only of a Rook should be sufficient to bring an easy victory. It is when pieces of similar value, say Bishops, or a Knight and a Bishop, are exchanged, that the resulting difference between the position before and after exchanging becomes all important.

When is it advisable to exchange? There are a number of circumstances in which exchanging is advisable, and the most important of these are listed below.

(1) When up in material.

In almost every case, when, say, a piece up, the ultimate winning of the game is made easier by exchanging as many pieces as possible. If you are a piece up, then obviously, if you have two pieces to his one, it will be easier to win than if you have five pieces to his four, just as the ratio 2–1 is greater than 5–4.

Note that this applies to exchange of pieces, not pawns. It is seldom advisable to exchange the pawns, since it is the player down in pieces who will have the difficult task of defending those pawns against superior forces.

(2) To gain material.

When an exchange, or series of exchanges, would result in a gain of material, unless your position is weakened to an extent greater than the value of your gain in material, you should make the exchange or exchanges.

A simple case is shown in diagram 97.

White by playing 1 Q×Q, Kt×Q can win the black pawn.

Diagram 97

(3) For tactical considerations.

(a) To get rid of attacking pieces when defending.

(b) To get rid of obstructing defenders when attacking.

(c) To liquidate and ease the tension when in a difficult, and likely to be disadvantageous, position.

(a) When you are being subjected to a vigorous attack, if you can get rid of some of the more active attacking pieces by exchanging for them defending pieces of similar value, the attack is less likely to succeed. In addition, the greater manœuvrability of the attacking pieces makes them a valuable prize.

Diagram 98

Diagram 99

*Example* (diagram 98). With Black to move, he has a very powerful attack by 1 ... R×R; 2 R×R, Kt–Kt4. But with White to move, by playing 1 Q–B5, he forces the exchange of Queens (since the Knight is otherwise lost), and after 1 ... Q×Q, Kt×Q Black's attack is completely broken up.

(*b*) When you are conducting an attack, however, it may well be necessary to exchange off some defending piece which is holding it up.

*Example* (diagram 99). Here White is attacking along the QKt1–KR7 diagonal, but this attack cannot be brought home because of the black Knight at KB3. Therefore the Knight must be removed, the line of play being 1 Kt×Kt *ch*, Kt×Kt. Now there still remains a Knight at Black's KB3, so 2 B×Kt. Now, when Black recaptures, e.g. 2 . . . B×B; 3 Q×P mate.

But remember that though it may be a good idea in a number of circumstances, often you may be furthering your opponent's cause, since normally he wishes to exchange his defenders against your attackers.

Remember, also, that a highly manœuvrable piece is on top of his form, and you may be exchanging him for a player well past his prime, who can no longer get about the field, as he did in days of yore!

(*c*) If your pieces are cramped and lack space for manœuvring, then clearly the fewer there are the more space each individual piece will have. Consequently, exchanging may often be advantageous when in a cramped position.

(4) To create the weaknesses and positional factors previously mentioned.

*Example* (diagram 100). In this position White's 1 B×B' P×B creates two isolated pawns in Black's position, and an open file commanded by White's Rook.

(5) To gain a tempo.

Sometimes, particularly in the opening, it is useful to exchange in order to gain a tempo, as in our old example illustrated again in diagram 101.

*Diagram 100*

*Diagram 101*

After 1 P×P, Q×P; 2 Kt–QB3, White has gained a tempo by the original pawn exchange.

(6) For end-game considerations.

One of the commonest examples of this is in exchanging in order to obtain Bishops of oppo-site colour to get a drawn ending. Examine the position in diagram 102.

White is to play. His position does not look very good. But White plays 1 Kt–Kt6 *ch*, K–B3; 2 Kt×B having Bishops of opposite colour and a drawn game. (The white Bishop by moving up and down the dia-gonal on which it stands,

*Diagram 102*

prevents the black King's pawn from moving forward without being lost, and thus the white King cannot be dislodged.)

But, by playing immediately 1 Kt×B, White would lose, since then Black's "white square" Bishop would be able to assist in the fight for the advancement of the pawns.

*Note.* There is one aspect of exchanging, which must be mentioned for the sake of completeness, but which is not strictly speaking, within the scope and objects of this book—THE SACRIFICE.

An exchange is considered a sacrifice, when a piece of high value is exchanged for one of lower value, with the object (generally within a few moves) of regaining all the lost material plus "interest on the loan" or else achieving mate.

The ability to make successful sacrifices (unsuccessful or "unsound" ones are, alas, all too common!) requires imagination, an ability to visualize the position several moves ahead, and chess experience.

The aim of this book is to teach the basic principles of chess play, and if the reader exchanges in accordance with the advice given in this chapter, the occasions when a brilliant sacrifice on the part of his opponent upsets his plans, will be very much more the exception than the rule.

Summary—The Inter-dependence of the Minor Strategic Conceptions

It is worth recalling and noting before we pass on to Higher Strategy, that all these minor strategic conceptions—The Pawns and their Weaknesses; The Open File and Seventh Rank; Pinning and Exchanging, are inter-dependent, or interchangeable one with another.

The two main points which should not be forgotten in this connexion are—

(1) These minor strategic conceptions are *not* a collection of single items, each one endowed with a virtue peculiarly its own, but in the words of the poet Alexander Pope—

"All are but part of one stupendous whole"

And if we may be allowed to paraphrase the second line we may continue—

"Whose body pieces are, and Chess the Soul"

(2) They are, therefore, not ends in themselves, but a means to an end—the higher strategy governing the conduct of your whole game of chess.

It is not sufficient to toil with great cunning, and finally force, say, an isolated pawn upon your opponent, and then sit back contentedly, awaiting his resignation. That isolated pawn is merely a weapon to assist you in your plan for winning your whole game.

And it is with this Higher Strategy and Planning that the next section is concerned.

## HIGHER STRATEGY AND TACTICS

As we have said, the minor strongpoints and strategical conceptions which occur during the course of games are only a means to an end, the instruments with which to inflict a defeat on your opponent. They may well be described as uses of the weapons, but it is the Commander-in-Chief who must supply the overall plan for conducting the campaign.

That it is of vital importance for the C.-in-C. to have a good understanding of all the weapons at his disposal cannot be disputed, and we shall now see how they may be, one and all, used in support of that higher consideration—the plan for conducting the game as a whole.

The player who really understands chess has, from before he makes his first move, a plan of campaign, a plan, however, which will for the time being cover only the opening stages.

The first plan is to develop the pieces as centrally as possible, without loss of time, and with the object of gaining as great a control of the centre of the board as the opponent will allow.

When development has been completed, what next? It will be remembered that when assessing the position on finishing this opening stage, the game is likely to fall roughly into one of three categories—

(1) Opponent not developed.

(2) Opponent developed, but weak centrally.

(3) Opponent developed centrally as you are—position equal.

In case (1), it has been shown that with correct play thereafter you should obtain a winning game. The "higher" strategy required might be summed up as "attack with your fully developed pieces and win."

Since the centre is the most important part of the board, you have the advantage in case (2). How then is this advantage to be exploited?

Now in all three cases there are two main lines of action which may be employed against an opponent after completing your development, namely—

(a) Attack in the centre.

(b) Attack on a wing.

Your overall plan of campaign should be thought out with one or other of these possibilities as your ultimate aim, even if the attack cannot be made immediately.

### (a) Attack in the Centre

If it can be successfully achieved, an attack in the centre and a subsequent breakthrough there, is the ideal method of winning the game. In case (2) above, when your opponent is developed but weak centrally this can usually be brought about.

The centre is a better site for an attack than on the wing, because a breakthrough there gives three possible directions in which the forces can fan out, or the breakthrough be exploited, whereas a wing attack has the choice of only two directions in which to continue.

In connexion with the following diagrams, note again "Control of the Centre," page 7.

In diagram 103, the dispositions of the White and Black forces are represented at the stage when development is complete.

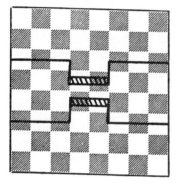
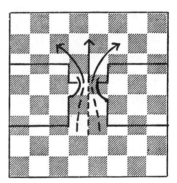

*Diagram 103*          *Diagram 104*

Remember that the marked areas may not necessarily indicate the actual position of the pieces, but rather the pressure the pieces are exerting on those areas. For the purposes of the ensuing explanations, we have divided the forces into "centre" and "wing" forces.

Now let us suppose the White Commander starts an attack in the centre. If a breakthrough occurs, there are three main directions (indicated by the arrows) along which the attack might continue, or indeed the White forces may fan out in all three directions (diagram 104).

Black would indeed be in a quandary in the event of such a breakthrough.

## (*b*) ATTACK ON A WING

If, as for instance in case (3) when your opponent is equally strong in the centre, it is not possible to attack successfully there, the other main strategy would be an attack on a wing.

In this connexion, since the capture of the King is the ultimate object of the game, the attack would probably be more dangerous if directed on the wing to which the opposing King had castled.

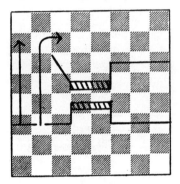

*Diagram 105*

In diagram 105 we see depicted an attack on a wing by White's forces. As can be seen, other things being equal, this would normally be inferior to a central attack, since there are only two main directions in which such an attack may fan out, as against three for an attack in the centre. It is thus easier for your opponent to cope with a wing attack and, in addition as we know, the individual pieces, such as the Knights and Bishops, will have less mobility than if they were taking part in a central attack.

### DEALING WITH A WING ATTACK

When your opponent is faced with a central attack he has little alternative but to try his utmost to hold up such an attack *in the centre*, by exchanging, blockading and any other means at his disposal. We have seen that a (counter) attack on the wing is unlikely to be so dangerous to you as your centre attack is to him. But in the case of a wing attack there is one excellent means of robbing it of its sting, and that is to *counter-attack in the centre*.

In diagram 106 we see that White has launched a wing attack, but Black by counter-attacking in the centre has broken through there. Apart from the likelihood that Black's attack is now the more menacing, he is also able to cross to that wing and cut off some of the White forces which are conducting the attack. The arrows indicate these possibilities.

It follows, therefore, that when you have not the necessary superiority to launch a successful attack in the centre, but have chances with one on a wing, *it is most essential to see that your centre is, and remains, sufficiently strong to prevent your opponent*

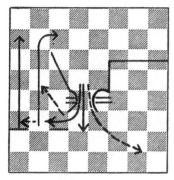

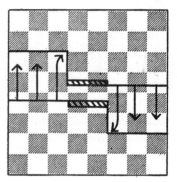

Diagram 106               Diagram 107

*replying with a successful central attack.* This may be done by maintaining the necessary forces there, or possibly by what is known as "blocking" the centre. This is similar to a blockade, as is done in the case of backward isolated pawns, but will be illustrated later.

Even if a counter-attack is not possible in the centre, your opponent has another main resource against a wing attack, and that is *a counter-attack on the opposite wing*.

If you have a larger force on one wing, and the centre is equal, it follows that your opponent will almost certainly have a larger force on the opposite wing. His attack may prove to be just that little bit more dangerous than yours, and thus turn the tide against you. A counter-attack on the opposite wing is particularly good when there has been heterogeneous castling, with the Kings in opposite corners of the board. In this case your wing attack against his King may be countered by an attack against your King.

In diagram 107 we see the wing countered by wing attack.

## COMPLEX ATTACKS

Sometimes, though your real objective may be an attack in the centre, this may best be achieved by first making a "feint," or preparatory attack on one wing. The object being to induce your opponent to divert some of his forces to that, or the opposite wing (if he plans to counter attack there), and consequently weaken his centre just sufficiently to allow you to make a successful central attack. Conversely, it may be a good idea first to make a feint in the centre, before thrusting home a final wing attack. These ideas will be illustrated amongst the actual chess positions which follow.

## DIFFERENT TYPES OF CENTRE

In the examples which follow mention will often be made of different types of centre positions—even centres, fluid centres,

*Diagram* 108

and locked centres. To illustrate the meaning of these terms simply, the following skeleton diagrams are appended.

### Even Centre

In diagram 108 the centre square control is even, but either side can advance or otherwise prepare to exert greater control in that centre as, for instance, if one or the other plays P–Q4. It is therefore also a *Fluid Centre*.

*Locked Centre*

In diagram 109 the pawns block one another and cannot advance. Thus to break through this type of centre would require considerable preliminary manœuvring, if it were possible at all.

## ATTACK IN THE CENTRE

This, if it can be accomplished successfully, is the ideal method of conducting the game.

This position (diagram 110) comes under case (2) if we associate

*Diagram 109*

*Diagram 110*

ourselves with the White forces—both developed, but opponent weaker centrally. White is able to play P–Q4, whereas Black cannot do so without loss of material. Assess the position for yourself, and see if you agree.

White, therefore, decides to attack and try to break through *in the centre.* So we have—

### 1  P–Q4

Now it is not proposed to go into an elaborate analysis of all possible moves. The object of this book is to deal with principles, not analysis, and so any analysis which is done is only to show the working of these underlying principles, and the reader is asked to bear that in mind throughout all the following illustrations.

However, it is clear that Black has two main lines of reply—

    (*a*)  1  ...          B–Kt3 (retiring before the attack)

or  (*b*)  1  ...          P×P (*or* B×P) (trying to break it up).

Now if he retires against the attack we have the following probable continuation—

(a)

| | |
|---|---|
| 1 ... | B–Kt3 |
| 2 P×P | |

pressing on with the centre attack.

| | |
|---|---|
| 2 ... | P×P |
| 3 B×KP | |

threatening 4 ... B×KKtP.

| | |
|---|---|
| 3 ... | Kt×B |
| 4 Q×Kt | Q×Q |
| 5 Kt×Q | |

This leads up to the position illustrated.

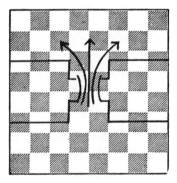

*Diagram* 111

*Diagram* 112

White has broken through in the centre. He commands the open central Queen's file, and because of his central position threatens to attack in any of the three directions.

Returning to diagram 110, if

1   P–Q4   P×P we have again two main lines of play.

(*b*)

| (1) | | (2) | |
|-----|-----|-----|-----|
| 2  B×P | | 2  B×P | Kt–K4 |

threatening B×P(Kt7).

| | | |
|---|---|---|
| 2 | ... | B×B |
| 3 | Q×B | R–Q1 |

In either case White can still break through in the centre and thus attain a winning position. For instance—

(1)

4  Q–Kt6

Utilizing one of the three direction possibilities of the centre attack. Now the breakthrough is complete, as Black cannot prevent loss of the Queen's pawn at least.

### ATTACK ON THE WING

We have already seen the complications arising from the possibilities of a wing attack. The position diagram 113 illustrates all these possibilities. Examine this position. *Black to move.*

(2)

| 3 | B×Kt | P×B |
|---|------|-----|
| 4 | Q×P  | Q×Q |
| 5 | Kt×Q |     |

*Diagram* 113

*Wing Attack with "Fluid" Centre*

It can be seen that Black is able to launch a very threatening wing attack by

$$1 \quad \ldots \qquad\qquad\qquad Kt \times KtP$$

What is White to do? His position does not look very good on that wing, but in any case the first thing to look for is any chances of counter-attack in the centre. Yes, there are such chances. So White's reply is

$$2 \quad P \times P\,!$$

If Black perseveres with his wing attack we get

$$2 \quad \ldots \qquad\qquad\qquad Kt \times R$$
$$3 \quad P \times R \qquad\qquad\qquad R\text{–}KB2$$

arriving at the position in diagram 115.

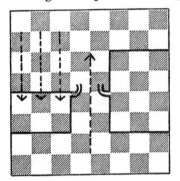

*Diagram 114*

*Diagram 115*

White's counter-attack in the centre has broken through, and now 4 P–Q7, must win, since the Rook cannot take because of the mate threat. If, however, Black does not altogether ignore the centre counter-attack, we may still have something like this—

$$1 \quad \ldots \qquad\qquad\qquad Kt \times KtP$$
$$2 \quad P \times P \qquad\qquad\qquad R\text{–}K3$$
$$3 \quad P \times P \qquad\qquad\qquad B\text{–}B2$$

| 4 | R–Kt7 | Kt × R |
|---|-------|--------|
| 5 | Kt–Kt5 | |

with an almost certain win.

*Wing Attack with "Locked" Centre*

But how much simpler it would have been if Black instead of attacking immediately on the wing, had first made sure he was safe from a counter-attack in the centre. In the original position he could have played—

| I | ... | P–K5 |
|---|-----|------|

With this move he locks the centre. In other words, he plays

*Diagram 116*

so that the centre becomes "fixed" rather than fluid, making it extremely difficult for either side to do anything there. Now the white Knight must move as well, so we might have the following variation—

| I | ... | P–K5 |
|---|-------|--------|
| 2 | Kt–Q2 | Kt × KtP |

and Black's wing attack now prevails.

*Wing Attack Countered by Attack on the Opposite Wing*

In the position shown in diagram 117 it will be seen that

Black has a strong attack against White's King's wing. Against the threat of Q–R7 *ch*, K–B1; Q–R8 *ch*, White is obliged to keep his Queen on its present diagonal so plays—

1    Q × RP

*Diagram* 117

with an eye on the possibility of counter-action on the Queen's side.

| | | |
|---|---|---|
| 1 | ... | R–Q6 |
| 2 | Kt–Q2 | R × Kt |

Black sacrifices his Rook in order to further his King's side attack.

| | | |
|---|---|---|
| 3 | B × R | Q–R7 *ch* |
| 4 | K–B1 | P–B6 |

White's position on the King's wing appears hopeless.
He has only one resource—*counter-attack on the opposite wing.*

| | | |
|---|---|---|
| 5 | Q–R8 *ch* | K–Q2 |
| 6 | Q–R4 *ch* | P–B3 |
| 7 | R–K7 *ch* ! ! | K × R |
| 8 | B–Kt5 *ch* | K–Q2 |
| 9 | R–Q1 *ch* | K–B2 |
| 10 | Q–R5 *ch* | K–Kt1 |
| 11 | Q–K5 *ch* | K–R1 |

| 12 | Q×R *ch* | K–R2 |
| 13 | Q–Q4 *ch* | P–Kt3 |
| 14 | K–K1 *!* | P×P |
| 15 | B–K3 | P–B4 |
| 16 | Q–K5 | P–Kt8(Q) *ch* |
| 17 | B×Q | Q×B *ch* |
| 18 | K–Q2 | Q–B7 *ch* |

Black still has his superiority on this side of the board, but White's counter-attack on the opposite side has succeeded in its objective.

| 19 | B–K2 | P–Kt7 |
| 20 | Q–K7 *ch* | K–Kt1 |
| 21 | Q–K3 | *Resigns* |

COMPLEX ATTACKS—PRELIMINARY ATTACK IN CENTRE LEADING
    TO WING ATTACK

In the position given in diagram 118, White has as his ultimate

*Diagram* 118

objective an attack on the King's wing. But first he makes a preliminary attack in the centre, since a direct wing attack could easily be nullified. So we get—

|   | 1 | BP×P | P×P |

2   P×P                    B×P
3   Kt–K3

With this last move White attacks the central black Bishop, which has become pinned as a result of White's centre attack. Note here the use to which this, and the subsequent pin are put —weapons to aid the overall plan, the final wing attack.

Black must get out of the pin or else lose the Bishop, so, plays

3   ...                    Q–Kt2

retaining the Queen in defence of the Bishop.

4   Kt–B5 *!*

The real object of White's manœuvre is now seen. The Wing attack is revealed.

4   ...                    P–B3

Forced, to prevent mate, but now the black Bishop is pinned again.

5   R–Kt3

The flank attack is strengthened. Now if 5 ... P–Kt3; 6 Q×P with an overwhelming position. So he plays

5   ...                    R–Q2
6   Q×P                    See diagram 119

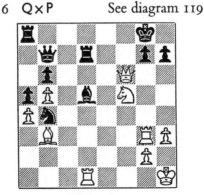

*Diagram* 119

Position after White's 6 Q×P

White's wing attack is now very powerful, with the threat of
7 R×B, Kt×R; 8 R×P *ch*, R×R; 9 B×Kt *ch*. Black has
possible defences, but none are sufficient to give him equality.
For example if

|        | 6  | ...        | R–KB1  |
|--------|----|------------|--------|
|        | 7  | Kt–R6 *ch* | K–R1   |
|        | 8  | Q×R *ch*   | B–Kt1  |
|        | 9  | Q×B *mate* |        |
| Or if  |    |            |        |
|        | 6  | ...        | R–KB2  |
|        | 7  | B×B        | Kt×B   |
|        | 8  | Kt–R6 *ch* | K–B1   |
|        | 9  | Q–Q6 *ch*  | R–K2   |
|        | 10 | R×Kt       |        |

and wins.

We have thus two main ideas to govern our approach to the
middle stage of the game. Attack in the centre, the ideal, as the
centre is the most important area of the board, but if that is not
possible, then an attack on one or other wing.

But do not get the idea that you must attack at all costs in
order to win the game, particularly when you have just finished
developing. As in warfare, an attack needs careful preparation,
and it is unwise to attack until your preparations are properly
complete. But there is your plan.

(1) Assess the position, and decide if you can successfully
attack in the centre. If not, then on one or other wing.

(2) Make all preparations necessary for the attack, seeing that
your pieces are all well placed in the light of the decision you
make.

(3) Carry out the planned attack.

Now it is quite possible that while you are carrying out the preparations for your attack, the opponent may launch an attack of his own.

If that attack comes in the centre, then it must be stopped at all costs. If you have developed correctly there is no danger that you will be weaker in the centre than your opponent, so by careful play such an attack should be stopped, if not thrown back with heavy losses to the attacker. If the attack comes on the wing, the first thing to do is to see if your opponent has weakened his centre, or, whether he has or not, if you can *counter-attack in the centre.*

If you can, then that is almost invariably the best reply. If not, examine the possibilities of a counter-attack on the opposite wing. But, in either case, always pay attention to his attack, never ignore it. There are times when, even with a superior centre, it is essential to bring a wing attack to a halt on that wing.

### When in a Poor Position

The reader, in spite of his diligent perusal of this book (!), will occasionally find that he has a very poor position. You may find—

(1) Yourself undeveloped.

(2) Yourself developed, but weak centrally.

*Yourself Undeveloped.* If you should find that for some reason or other you have failed to develop, while your opponent has done so, there are two important things to do in these circumstances.

(a) Develop!!

(b) Do *not* open up the game and try all in your power to prevent your opponent doing so. He will be trying to attack and win with the pieces, and the less you open up the game the more difficult it will be for those pieces to penetrate into your position. (See "Open and Close Games" in the games section.)

*Yourself Developed, but Weak Centrally.* In this case there are again two important considerations to bear in mind, namely—

(*a*) Transfer all the forces you can to bear on to the centre squares.

(*b*) Do not open up the game.

If the game becomes open, your opponent will be more likely to be able to advance in the all-important centre, and in addition his pieces there will have the greater mobility.

### CONCLUSION

In the matter of selecting one's higher strategy for conducting each game, it is one's chess judgment which must decide which to adopt.

As the authors have previously remarked, the knowledge you will acquire from reading this book will "give you the tools." You must "finish the job."

### *Summary*

The main features of the Higher Strategy can be summarized in the form of a tree, which is appended here for the convenience of the reader.

## YOUR DEVELOPMENT COMPLETE

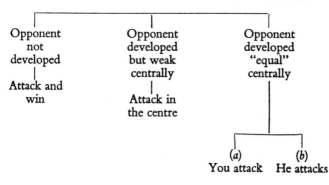

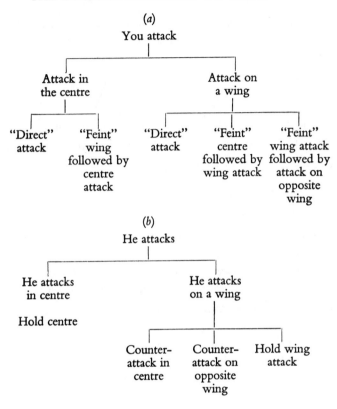

## CHAPTER IV

# The End-game

WHAT is meant by an End-game? Does every game have an end-game? The answer to the second question is very definitely "No." Taking it in its most absurd form, we could have the following game—

| | | |
|---|---|---|
| 1 | P–KB4 | P–K3 |
| 2 | P–KKt4 | Q–R5 *mate* |

It would be very difficult to find more than the opening stage in that game!

The same applies though to all games in which mate occurs with many pieces on the board. What is it then, that makes the end part of a game an "end-game"?

The two salient features of an end-game are—

(1) A change in the value of the pawns.

(2) A change in value of the King.

As soon as the time arrives when the pawns become "transformed" from mere infantrymen to potential Queens, then the game has become an end-game.

Concurrently with this, the King usually sheds his role of a piece needing protection and best kept away from the height of the battle, and becomes a source of strength, both in attack and defence, and indeed a potential match winner, fully worthy of his crown!

The end-game, however, is in some respects different from the opening and middle-game. If chess is both an art and a science, then it is in the end-game that the science is most pronounced.

Very often indeed the ending might be decided on simple mathematics, as, for instance, if your opponent can Queen his pawn in five moves, but yours can get home in three.

## THE PASSED PAWN

A pawn is considered "passed" when on its own file, or either of the adjacent files, there are no opposing pawns between it and the eighth rank.

In diagram 120 we have a simple illustration of a passed pawn

*Diagram* 120

—Black's Queen's Bishop's pawn. Its march to the eighth rank cannot be interfered with by the white pawns. Neither of the white pawns, however, is a passed pawn.

If a pawn is a potential Queen, a passed pawn is very much further on the road to becoming an *actual* Queen, since there are no opposing pawns to prevent it from marching straight down the board and reaching the eighth rank. Thus the basic mechanism for transforming a potential Queen into an actual Queen is to create a passed pawn and march the passed pawn down to the eighth rank, when it can be exchanged for a Queen or any other piece the player may choose.

So the next question naturally is—How can a passed pawn be created?

*Every healthy pawn majority is capable of producing a passed pawn.*

The meaning of the word "healthy" in this connexion is that the majority pawns are not exhibiting any pawn weaknesses— such as doubled pawns or backward pawns. The importance of this factor will be seen later in the chapter. Examine the pawn position in diagram 121.

The correct play for White to obtain a passed pawn from a healthy pawn majority is to *advance the unopposed pawn.*

Thus White would play 1 P–B4. Assuming the play is confined to these pawns Black might reply 1 ... P–Kt3. Now after 2 P–Kt4, P–R3; 3 P–B5, a passed pawn appears. If after 1 P–B4 Black's reply is P–R4 (in order to block temporarily the advance of White's Knight's pawn), then

2 P–Kt3 (P–R3? P–R5!), P–Kt3; 3 P–R3, P–R5; 4 P–Kt4, and Black cannot avoid P–B5 resulting in a passed pawn as previously. Thus a pawn majority without any basic weaknesses will always produce a passed pawn, but only with correct play, and the guiding rule is—*advance the unopposed pawn.*

*Diagram* 121

In the case of a healthy pawn majority it is nearly always possible to create a passed pawn without allowing your opponent to do the same. But in the case of an unhealthy pawn majority, or pawn equality that may not be possible, and so we have these two factors to bear in mind—

(1) Creation of a passed pawn. Can I create a passed pawn?

(2) March of the passed pawn to the eighth rank. Will my passed pawn reach it before my opponent's?

### Unhealthy Pawn Majorities

From our definition of healthy pawn majorities it follows that unhealthy ones are those which exhibit the characteristic weaknesses of formation explained in the sections on pawns in the middle-game.

These unhealthy formations may be divided into those which

can create a passed pawn, and those which cannot. For example, in diagram 122 below—

*Diagram* 122

Here Black has a majority of three pawns to two, but owing to the doubled pawn formation the creation of a passed pawn is not possible by the pawns themselves.

In the next diagram (123), however, White has a pawn majority both on the King's and the Queen's sides. Both these majorities can create a passed pawn, on the Queen's side by P–R4 or P–B4, and the King's side by 1 P–B5, and if 1 ... P×P; 2 P–Kt6, P×P; 3 P–R7. The essential difference, however, lies in the respective positions of the pawns.

In each case Black also obtains a passed pawn by P×P *e.p.*

*Diagram* 123

or P×P, but whereas on the King's side White's pawn would queen first, on the other side Black would do so.

"Can I create a passed pawn?" From White's viewpoint the answer on both sides of the board is "Yes."

"Will my passed pawn queen before my opponent?" On the King's side "Yes," on the Queen's side "No."

## *Pawn Equalities*

Pawn equalities unable to produce a passed pawn are too common to require mention. Cases where the passed pawn can be created from pawn equality fall into two categories. In the first of these, the opponent has already a passed pawn, or can create one. This idea is really the same as that of an unhealthy pawn majority, the majority being on *one side* of the formation.

For instance, in the position shown in diagram 124, Black already has a passed pawn on the King's side, but owing to the position of the pawns White holds the advantage after P–R6.

The second, and most important case occurs when there is no passed pawn already created, and no "pawn majority" balance on either side of the pawn formations. This applies to the Queen's side pawns in diagram 124.

*Diagram* 124

Can White create a passed pawn? The answer is "Yes." Will that passed pawn reach the eighth rank before any passed pawn of Black's? Again the answer is "Yes." But viewed from Black's angle, though the answer to (1) is "Yes," the answer to (2) is "No." To create a passed pawn from this position—*advance the centre pawn*.

1 P–Kt6. If either of Black's side pawns move forward, White simply plays 2 P×P and his (ex) KtP is passed. So Black must take. If 1 ... RP×P; 2 P–B6! If 1 ... BP×P; 2 P–R6! Following one side of the symmetrical position 1 P–Kt6, RP×P; 2 P–B6. Now if 2 ... P×RP; 3 P×KtP and White has his passed pawn; if 2 ... P×BP; 3 P–R6 and the pawn is passed. Note, of course, that Black has in either case no less than three passed pawns. Thus unless White's single pawn can queen first the game is lost.

*Sacrifice of Pieces*

The position in diagram 125 shows a simple, but by no means uncommon example of the sacrifice as a medium for creating a

passed pawn.   1  B×P,  P×B and White's Knight's pawn is passed.   Such a sacrifice is obviously well rewarded, with Queen instead of Bishop as a result.

To summarize so far.  We have two factors to consider in the matter of queening a pawn.

(1)  Create a passed pawn.

*Diagram 125*

(2)  Ensure that the passed pawn so created reaches the eighth rank before any passed pawn of your opponent's.

The next important factor to consider concerns the Kings.

## THE KING IN RELATION TO PASSED PAWNS—THE "SQUARE RULE"

In diagram 126 we see a white passed pawn and a black King. Can the King arrest the march of this pawn to the eighth rank?

Now imagine a square whose sides are equal to the distance from this passed pawn to its eighth rank, including for this assessment the square on which the pawn stands.  Thus in this case the square is 5 chess squares by 5, with the pawn in the

*Diagram 126*

bottom left corner.  This imaginary square is indicated by the broken line in this diagram.

The rule is—*If the King can get inside the square thus formed by the pawn, the pawn can be stopped from queening.* Thus if it is Black's move he plays 1 ... K–K5 (indicated by a cross), and thus being inside the square can stop the pawn. Try it out. But on the other hand, if it were White's move, he could play 1 P–R5, and the all-important square would be now "4 by 4" marked by the continuous line in the diagram. Now the black King cannot move into that square with his move, so the pawn gets home.

There are two "catches" in relation to this square rule worthy of mention. Both are illustrated in diagram 127. The square of the white passed pawn is "4 by 4" but it can extend *either to the right or left.* Thus whether the black King be at KR5 or QR5 it can still get inside the vital square if it is Black's move. The second "catch" point is that the King must be able to get into the square of the pawn *and stay in the square of the pawn.* Thus the black King at KR5 could not, in fact, catch the white pawn.

*Diagram 127*

Though with his first move (K–Kt4) he gets inside the square, after 2 P–Q6, he cannot now get inside the new "3 by 3" square, as his progress is blocked by his own pawn, and after moving the pawn he is too late, as the square will be reduced to "2 by 2" with White's next move. Note also that a pawn on its second rank can move two squares, and in that case the square must be calculated as if the pawn were on the third rank.

We have now considered the King in relation to one passed pawn. Owing to its power of being able to move in any direction, the King is often able to hold up more than one passed pawn.

THE KING IN RELATION TO TWO PASSED PAWNS

In this connexion there are two possibilities to be considered,

(1) Two distant passed pawns.

(2) Two united passed pawns.

(1) In diagram 128 is shown a black King in relation to two

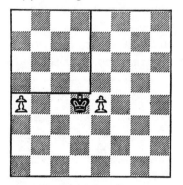

Diagram 128

distant passed pawns. If Black had the move he would be able to play 1 ... K×P and after 2 P–R5, the King can still stop the other pawn. If, however, White is to move, what then is the correct play? *Not* 1 P–K5, as after 1 ... K×P Black is still able to catch the Rook's pawn.

But after 1 P–R5 what is Black to do? If 1 ... K×P; 2 P–R6, and he can no longer get inside the vital square. If 1 ... K–B4, Black has merely postponed the evil day of deciding which of the pawns he must go for, and White is bound to get one or the other home. The simplest way to force this would be 2 P–R6, K–Kt3; 3 P–K5, K×P; 4 P–K6 and the black King is outside. If the black King merely marks time and goes for neither pawn, they can be moved up alternately and he cannot deal with both at once. The general rule then in this type of case is—*Move the pawn which is farthest from the opposing King.*

(2) In the case of united passed pawns there are distinct differences. United passed pawns have both advantages and disadvantages compared with distant passed pawns. In diagram 129, for instance, a disadvantage is that unassisted neither can queen, but an advantage is that the King cannot take either pawn, since the front one is protected, while if the rear one is

captured the front one can then queen. This applies to whatever position on the board they may occupy, and the opposing King is tied down to stopping their advance and cannot take part in any other operations. But their advance *can* be held up. Here the King merely has to play to K2 and then back again to Q3.

*Diagram 129*

*Diagram 130*

Another factor which may sometimes be a disadvantage, in the case of united passed pawns, occurs when Black also has a suitable pawn. Imagine a black pawn at QB2.

Again the King cannot take the rear pawn, but is able to play 1 ... P–B3! Now after 2 P×P, and whichever pawn the King takes he is still able to capture the other one. It is apparent, therefore, that in an end-game with King and pawns, distance is as important a factor as protection, for passed pawns.

To illustrate clearly the importance of distant passed pawns, in comparison with united ones in an end-game, here is a simple example—

In diagram 130 White (to play) has two united passed pawns, Black two distant ones. After 1 P–K4, though the white King can easily catch either of the black pawns, he cannot catch both. For example—

|   |        |      |
|---|--------|------|
| 1 | P–K4   | P–R4 |
| 2 | P–K5 *ch* | K–K2 |

|   |         |      |
|---|---------|------|
| 3 | P–Q5    | P–B6 |
| 4 | K–K3    |      |

Forced, otherwise the Bishop's pawn gets home.

|   |          |      |
|---|----------|------|
| 4 | ...      | P–R5 |
| 5 | P–Q6 *ch* | K–K3 |
| 6 | *Resigns* |      |

The mobility of the united pawns is spent, and though the white King is inside the "square" of both the black pawns, he cannot capture both and one must get home.

### KING AND PAWN AGAINST KING—THE OPPOSITION

It cannot be too strongly emphasized that the technique to be employed in queening a single passed pawn when the opposing King can prevent its unaided march to the eighth rank, is of vital importance in almost every end-game. When this technique is thoroughly understood, confidence in the end-game stage will follow automatically.

Not that it is by any means always possible to obtain a Queen from a single remaining pawn. It depends on the relative positions of the Kings. In the diagram below is shown an *ideal* position for this purpose.

#### KING AND PAWN VERSUS KING—THE "IDEAL" POSITION FOR QUEENING

This illustration shows an ideal position for White to queen his pawn since, whoever has the move, queening is possible.

Note the position in diagram 131 carefully and observe that there are two characteristic features in connexion with it. They are—

(1) King *in front* of the passed pawn.

(2) A clear square between the King and its pawn.

It is not possible, with correct play on the opponent's part, to queen a single pawn unless your King can be brought in front of the passed pawn.

*Diagram 131*

Unless the King is at least two squares in front of its passed pawn, the queening of that pawn will depend *entirely* on who has the move.

Now from this "ideal" position the technique for queening the pawn is as under. The reader is advised to follow this on a chess board.

### The Opposition

In their present position the two Kings are said to be in OPPOSITION. This occurs when they are on the same file or diagonal with one square separating them. The opposition may appear as DISTANT OPPOSITION when there are three or five squares separating them. This simply means that on approaching one another they arrive in normal opposition *with the move still with the player who started the approach.* The significance of the opposition lies in this last point. Examine the position of the two Kings, ignoring momentarily the pawn. The King which has to move is forced to allow the other to advance if it wishes. Thus the side *not* having the move is said to *hold*, or *have, the opposition.* For instance, if Black is to move in this diagram he cannot prevent the white King reaching the eighth rank, should it need to get there. For instance, if Black plays 1 ... K–Q3; 2 K–B5, and merely by "regaining" the opposition at each alternate move the white King will eventually reach his eighth, e.g. 1 ... K–Q3; 2 K–B5, K–K2; 3 K–K5 regaining the opposition, but one step nearer the eighth! 3 ... K–Q1; 4 K–B6, K–K1; 5 K–K6. Now after 5 ... K–Q1 there is no redress for Black when White moves 6 K–B7. If, of course, Black plays 1 ... K–B3, then the symmetrical variation occurs on the other side after 2 K–Q5. If Black retreats directly by 1 ... K–K2, it is even simpler, 2 K–K5!

That then is the significance of what is known as the opposition. Let us now return to our original position and see how it helps in queening the pawn.

The importance of the square between the white King and its pawn is now clear. If White has the move, then as far as the Kings alone are concerned it is *Black* who has the opposition, and White's King can never move forward.

So, in order to queen from this position, and White having to move, he regains the opposition by 1 P–K3. Now there are only two distinct lines of play for Black. He may play partly the one and partly the other, but these two lines are to retire the King directly (1 ... K–K2) or to move to one side (... K–Q3 or K–B3).

(*a*) Firstly, the direct retirement

1     ...                    K–K2

White then follows up directly with,

2   K–K5

and once again we have the "ideal" position, with the difference that the white pawn is one square nearer the eighth rank. Now after

2   ...                    K–K1
3   K–K6

and now Black is compelled to move to one side or the other. The pawn can then be queened simply by

3   ...                    K–Q1
4   P–K4                   K–K1

The "ideal" position again.

|   |      |      |
|---|------|------|
| 5 | P–K5 | K–Q1 |
| 6 | K–B7 |      |

The *opposite* way to the black King's move (therefore if 5 ... K–B1; 6 K–Q7).

|   |                 |      |
|---|-----------------|------|
| 6 | ...             | K–Q2 |
| 7 | P–K6 *ch*       | K–Q1 |
| 8 | P–K7 *ch*       | K–Q2 |
| 9 | P–K8 (Queens) *ch* |   |

(*b*) The other direct line for Black after 1 P–K3 is the immediate sideways move, e.g.

|   |     |      |
|---|-----|------|
| 1 | ... | K–Q3 |

White will then immediately move forward in order to "pass" the black King with

|   |      |
|---|------|
| 2 | K–B5 |

(if 1 ... K–B3, 2 K–Q5). Now if 2 ... K–K2; 3 K–K5 transposing into the first variation and the "ideal" position again. So we can ignore all moves that transpose into variation (*a*).

After

|   |           |      |
|---|-----------|------|
| 2 | ...       | K–Q4 |
| 3 | P–K4 *ch* | K–Q3 |

Remember in this position always to keep the King in front of the pawn. The procedure, therefore, is *not* 4 P–K5 *ch* which would only produce a draw (see later), but

|   |      |
|---|------|
| 4 | K–B6 |

Now would follow

|   |      |      |
|---|------|------|
| 4 | ...  | K–Q2 |
| 5 | P–K5 |      |

(Note the King is still in front of the pawn.)
(*a*) Now if

|   |   |   |
|---|---|---|
| 5 | ... | K–K1 |

of course

|   |   |   |
|---|---|---|
| 6 | K–K6 | K–Q1 |
| 7 | K–B7 | K–Q2 |
| 8 | P–K6 *ch* | |

(*b*) If

|   |   |   |
|---|---|---|
| 5 | ... | (any other King move) |

then

|   |   |
|---|---|
| 6 | K–B7 |

followed by P–K6–7–8–Queen!

The reader is advised to study this technique very thoroughly and note that though it may at first sight seem very complicated, it is really essentially simple. Note that there are only two distinct variations, however much the two may be intermingled.

(1) *The Direct Retirement of the Opposing King.* Follow up directly, and move the pawn only when the ideal position is present, or is reached by movement of that pawn (e.g. when the pawn is three squares behind the King). On reaching his first rank the defending King is compelled to move to one side. Then advance the King diagonally in the opposite direction, after which the pawn can be run in.

(2) *The Side Movement of the Opposing King.* Advance diagonally in the opposite direction to which his King moved. *Always* keep ahead of the pawn, but when three squares ahead, the pawn can and should be moved up one square. Thus the difference between the King and pawn in "squares from the eighth rank" will be 3, 2, 3, 2, etc. When the King reaches the seventh rank the pawn can then be run in, since it will be protected and the opposing King can no longer occupy the pawn's eighth rank.

### KING AND PAWN VERSUS KING—THE "POSSIBLE" POSITION FOR QUEENING THE PAWN

The position shown in diagram 132 differs in one vital respect from the "ideal" position shown previously. Though the white King is in front of the pawn, there is no clear square between it and the pawn. Thus queening is possible, but depends *entirely on who has the move*. If Black is to move, then White holds the opposition. The black King must move and queening is therefore carried out with the technique employed from the "ideal" position. But if White has to move it is Black who holds the opposition, and with correct play can prevent White from queening. White *cannot advance his King*, since if 1 K–Q4, K–Q3 and if 1 K–B4, K–B3. So after

*Diagram 132*

$$1 \quad \text{K–Q4} \qquad\qquad \text{K–Q3}$$

White has no alternative but repetition of moves or else

$$2 \quad \text{P–K4}$$

(see diagram 134).

After this move it will be noted that the white King is no longer in front of the pawn, and can never again get in front, and cannot, therefore, queen it. Why this cannot be done will be shown from the next position.

### KING AND PAWN VERSUS KING—THE "IMPOSSIBLE" POSITION FOR QUEENING THE PAWN

The remaining distinct position with King and pawn against

King is shown in diagram 133. In this position *whoever* has the move, queening is not possible with correct play on Black's part. The essential condition that the white King gets in front of his

*Diagram 133*

pawn can never be achieved. From this position, therefore, it is necessary for the reader to understand the technique by which the lone King can prevent this pawn from queening. This position, therefore, will be examined from Black's angle.

Now the presence of the pawn does not alter the fact that the Kings are in opposition. If Black is to move, then it is White who has the opposition, but in either case after two moves the positions become identical.

For example—

| | White to move | | Black to move | |
|---|---|---|---|---|
| 1 | K–Q3 | K–K3 | 1 ... | K–K3 |
| 2 | K–Q4 | K–Q3 | 2 K–Q4 | K–Q3 |

Illustrated on page 115 (diagram 134).

Note that if the white King had come round the other side of the pawn it would simply mean that the Kings were at B4 and B3 instead of Q4 and Q3.

The technique for Black, if he has the move, *is to retire his King directly* and whichever way the white King moves, take up the "opposition."

White cannot advance the King as Black has the opposition. So White must play

|    | 3 | P–K5 *ch* | K–K3 |
|---|---|---|---|

and now White must abandon the pawn or else return to the "impossible" position with 4 K–K4. Now by

| 4 | ... | K–K2 |

Black compels the same procedure on White's part in order to advance his pawn at all, so we get

| 4 | ... | K–K2 |
| 5 | K–Q5 | K–Q2 |
| 6 | P–K6 *ch* | K–K2 |
| 7 | K–K5 | |

*Diagram* 134

Now after

| 7 | ... | K–K1 |
| 8 | K–Q6 | K–Q1 |

(the position again) White must play

| 9 | P–K7 *ch* |

in order to advance the pawn. Now after

| 9 | ... | K–K1 |

White must abandon the pawn or play

| 10 | K–K6 *stalemate !* |

If, in the position diagrammed above it were Black's move, and not White's, it would make no difference. Examine the above position again, with Black to move

|   |   |   |
|---|---|---|
| I | ... | K–K3 |

Preventing the white King from coming in front of the pawn. White must still advance the pawn, since after 2 K–K3 (or 2 K–Q3), we get 2 ... K–K4 and are back to the "impossible" position again. So White must try

|   |   |   |
|---|---|---|
| 2 | P–K5 | |

Now after

|   |   |   |
|---|---|---|
| 2 | ... | K–K2 |
| 3 | K–Q5 | K–Q2 |
| 4 | P–K6 *ch* | K–K2 |
| 5 | K–K5 | |

the same position as before, is reached.

Though it may seem complicated to begin with, the technique is again quite simple for Black to secure the draw. Always retire the King *directly* back from the pawn, and whichever way the opponent moves his King (the pawn cannot be advanced without its support), *regain the opposition*. This leads to a constant repetition of the original "impossible" position and when this occurs with the pawn on the seventh rank it is a STALEMATE.

The queening of a single passed pawn which cannot run home unaided depends then entirely on whether the ideal position can be reached, or the "possible" position reached with the lone King to move. Otherwise one pawn alone is insufficient to win an end-game.

It was noted in the previous chapter that two united passed pawns can be held up by an opposing King, but cannot be taken. With the assistance of their own King, however, one can always be made to queen.

In diagram 135 we see a position with two united white passed pawns. There is more than one way in which one of the pawns can be queened but the reader, knowing the technique for queening one pawn, could come to no harm by taking up the "ideal" position in relation to one or the other of these passed pawns. The black King is com- pelled to alternate between his K3 and Q2, so White would merely march the King up the board in the manner indicated, arriving at KKt6. Having reached there, if it is Black's move White already has the opposition and after say 1 ... K–Q2; 2 K–B7, the King's pawn can march in regardless of the Queen's pawn. If White has the

*Diagram 135*

move, the opposition can be gained by the simple sacrifice 1 P–Q7, K×P; 2 K–B7 and the King's pawn again runs in. This technique is simple and safe, even though there are other methods.

*Summary*

Understanding the importance of the position of the King in relation to the final pawn, makes it easy to know when, and when not to swop off, say, that final piece, should the oppor- tunity occur.

EXCEPTIONS TO THE BASIC MECHANISM

Before concluding this chapter, note must be made of two exceptions which occur in the BASIC MECHANISM of King and pawn against King. These are—

(1) When the passed pawn is on the Rook's file.

(2) When the attacking King has reached the sixth rank.

*The Pawn on a Rook's File*

The technique and ideal position for queening a pawn applies to all cases except when the pawn is on a Rook's file.

In diagram 136 is the ideal position shown with the pawn on

*Diagram 136*

the Rook's file. Now with

1    P–R5                    K–Kt1

the limits of the board prevent the vital move for White of the King advancing in the *opposite direction to Black's King's move*. White, therefore, has no alternative but

2    K–Kt6

So after

2    ...                    K–R1

White can do nothing to prevent a draw. If

3    P–R6

his King is no longer in front of his pawn and Black gains the opposition with 3 ... K–Kt1, and if

3    K–B7

the pawn is lost.

It is only in extremely favourable circumstances that a Rook's pawn can be queened when the lone King can get inside the pawn's "square" (Square Rule).

Two conditions are essential before such a pawn can be queened. The hostile King must be prevented—

(1) From reaching the queening square of the pawn.

(2) From reaching even the Bishop's file on the same side of the board and in front of the pawn.

*Diagram 137*

In diagram 137 the white King and pawn are in the "ideal" position, but Black's King has been able to reach the Bishop's file. The result is that White can never get his King off the Rook's file to allow the pawn to queen, and still keep the opposing King from reaching the queening square!

After 1 P–R6, K–B1; 2 K–R8, K–B2; (if, of course 1 P–R6, K–B1; 2 K–Kt6, *K–Kt1* as in the previous example).

*Diagram 138*

*Attacking King on the Sixth Rank*

In diagram 138 the "possible" position is shown when the white King is in front of the pawn, *and the pawn has reached the fifth rank*. In this position it is *always* possible for the pawn to be queened, even if it should be White's move. This is accomplished by pushing up the pawn an extra square in order to

regain the lost opposition. For example, 1 K–Q6, K–Q1; 2
P–B6, K–B1; 3 *P–B7* and the black King cannot move now to
Q1, so after 3 ... K–Kt2; 4 K–Q7 and wins.

## KING AND PAWNS AGAINST KING AND PAWNS

As was pointed out in the introduction, the distinguishing
features of the end-game lie in the change of value of the pawns
and the King.

Originally a piece needing protection, and best tucked away
in a corner, the King emerges in the ending as a more and more
powerful piece. When only pawns remain on the board, it
becomes the dominant factor in the game, both in attack and
defence. The King can have an indispensable part to play in
bringing home a passed pawn, yet even this was a supporting role.

However, when there are a number of pawns remaining, and
particularly if none are passed pawns, the King is seen as justly
meriting his crown! Remem-
bering that the value of the
pieces depends on their power
of movement, this must be so
because, though the King and
pawns can move only one square
at a time, the former can move
in any one of eight different
directions, while the latter must
plod always forward.

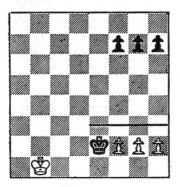

*Diagram* 139

The position in diagram 139
illustrates the supremacy of the
King very simply. Whoever has the move, the white pawns are
helpless against the attack of the black King, and Black must win.
(The King as an attacker.) Yet if the white King were at KKt1
instead of QKt1, the white pawns could no longer be touched
by the opposing King, and all would be well for White (King
as defender).

Nevertheless, the pawns are not altogether impotent against a King, and once again we come to note the inestimable value of STRONG PAWN-FORMATIONS.

Take the following position for instance (diagram 140).

In order to capture any of the white pawns Black is compelled to make four preliminary moves, owing to the "unbroken" front of four squares controlled by this pawn formation. Thus, even with Black to move, a white King at QR1 would stop the whole attack merely by playing K–Kt1 (or 2) and K–B2.

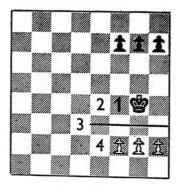

*Diagram 140*

If, however, the Bishop's pawn were played up one square making another of our well-known pawn-formations (diagram 141), the black King would require only three preliminary moves before being in a position

*Diagram 141*

*Diagram 142*

to capture one of the pawns. Note that even if White's King were on QKt1 he would now be unable to stop Black's entry into the heart of his pawns.

The next diagram (142) is self-explanatory, showing that with the white pawns arranged in this formation, Black's King can get at them in one move only.

The pawn chain, if White's Bishop's pawn were on B4, is equally ineffective against entry by the King.

Now there is one factor which must be remembered in conducting an end-game of this nature. The King being the dominating piece is best situated *in the centre*. But what is meant by the centre in this case? The centre of the board? Not necessarily. The King's powers of movement are limited to one square at a time, so unless he is situated on the extreme edge of the board, his movement is unaffected by his position.

The area of operations remaining in a King and pawns ending may be very limited, and the King should, therefore, be in the *centre of that limited area.*

The guiding principles in conducting endings with King and pawns are summarized below.

(1) The King is the most powerful piece.

Bring the King as quickly as possible to the centre of the area of operations. Remember that the OPPOSITION is very important in these types of games and *so move the King, and keep pawn moves in reserve* to regain the opposition if lost. (The man who has *not* got to move his King holds the opposition.)

(2) Look to your pawn formations.

Remember that a strong pawn-formation can prevent the opponent's King from infiltrating into your position. *Pawn moves cannot be retracted, whilst King moves often can.* In order to give the reader an idea of the problems that can arise, the authors have given below one example of a typical King and pawns ending.

Study diagram 143. Black to move. Make a list of the points

to be noted about this position and compare them with the observations that follow.

(1) Equal material on both sides.

(2) Black has a pawn majority on the King's side, White on the Queen's side.

(3) White's King is more centrally placed than Black's.

(4) Black has the move.

*Diagram 143*

Once again it must be emphasized that no elaborate analysis of the large number of possible moves will be given, but clearly Black has two different lines of play. He may advance the King's side pawns, in order to create a passed pawn, or else move the King and keep the pawn moves in reserve. Now let us suppose he decides to advance the King's side pawns. Play might then run as follows—

|   | 1 ... | P–R4 |

advancing the unopposed pawn.

|   |   |   |
|---|---|---|
| 2 | K–Q5 | P–KKt4 |
| 3 | K×P | P–R5 |
| 4 | P–B5 | P×P |

If 4 ... P–Kt4; 5 P–B6 wins.

|   |   |   |
|---|---|---|
| 5 | P–R5 | P–Kt5 |
| 6 | P–R6 | P–R6 |
| 7 | P×P | P–Kt6 |

If 7 ... P×P; 8 P–R7; 9 P–R8(Q). Preventing Black's 9 P–R8.

|   |   |   |
|---|---|---|
| 8 | P–R7 | P–Kt7 |

| 9 | P–R8(Q) | P–Kt8(Q) |
| 10 | Q–B8 *ch* | |

King must move back.

11    Q–Kt8 ch

winning Black's Queen.

Although there are a large number of variations in this theme, it is clear that Black, by playing his pawns and not his King, stands a very good chance of losing this game.

But supposing he plays his King, and keeps the pawn moves in reserve. Now after 1 ... K–K3, how is White to break through with his pawn majority on the Queen's side? If he gains the opposition with 2 K–K4, Black with his pawn moves in hand has every prospect of regaining it, and at the very least should draw.

From this single illustration then, we can see the importance of the advice previously given. White's King was originally in a somewhat better position than Black's, and therefore it was doubly important for Black to play his King first—to get it into a central position, and to keep the pawn moves in reserve.

### THE ROOK IN THE END-GAME

Of all the pieces, not even excepting the Queen, the Rook may well be considered the end-game "Specialist." Fewer pieces mean greater manœuvring space for those that are left, and more open lines. It is under these conditions that the Rook shows up in its most favourable light.

The chief characteristics of the Rook in the end-game may be summarized as under—

(1) Rook at the height of its manœuvring powers.

It is on the open lines that the Rook displays its full power.

(2) Two coloured effect of Rook.

A Rook can attack on both black and white coloured squares

simultaneously, sometimes a vitally important factor in the end-game. This ability is shared only with the Queen.

(3) Peculiar ability of the Rook in attacking pawns.

A Rook attacking on a rank of pawns is like the sudden appearance of a machine-gunner at one end of a slit trench. Some of the occupants may scramble away to safety, but the death-roll is sure to be heavy. Similarly when a Rook attacks pawns on a file, no movement of the pawn is an escape. Pawns can, however, by moving forward escape the attack of Bishop or Knight.

(4) Rook and King can mate against King.

This is vitally important when Rook, pawn and King are left against Rook and King. In the case of Bishop or Knight, and pawn against Bishop or Knight, the weaker side may well have the chance of sacrificing his piece for the lone pawn and thus of securing a draw. This cannot be done when a Rook remains.

(5) Rook's power to restrict the movement of the opponent's King.

The King, urgently needed in the end-game can never cross a file or rank controlled by an opposing Rook.

The Major Functions of the Rook in the End-game

There are three major, and often very diverse functions which the Rook may be called upon to perform in the end-game. It is by no means always easy to decide to which of these tasks your Rook should be put, and it is here that your "chess judgment" may be tested to the full. What are these functions?

*Rook on the Open File*

When there are many pawns still on the board, it is of paramount importance in nearly every case, to seize the most advantageous open file with the Rook. Here the Rook can

utilize to the full its powers of movement and possibly infiltrate
into the enemy position, attack his pawns on the rank, and often

*Diagram* 144

will also then be able to fulfil its
second major function, that of
restricting the opposing King.

In diagram 144 there is equal
material, but Black's Rook is on
the only open file. Now with
Black to play, he can bring such
pressure to bear on White's
pawns that the positional advantage can be turned into a
material one, by the following
play—

1   ...                    R–B5

attacking the backward pawn.

2   R–Q1                   R–B7

seizing the seventh rank, and attacking pawns.

3   R–Kt1                  R–Q7

Poor White!

Note that it would have been bad play for Black to have
immediately seized the seventh rank with 1 ... R–B7, because
his occupation would have been challenged by White playing
2 R–B2, *e.g.*, 1 . . . R–B7, 2 R–B2, R–B5, 3 R–Q2.

From this one example we can note three possible results of
seizing the open file. Attack on the opposing pawns, restriction
of the opponent's King, and restriction of his Rook to the
defensive.

### Restriction of the Opposing King

Though we know that this may occur as a result of seizure of
the open file, it can also be a major function of the Rook later
in the ending.

When there are few pawns left on the board, it becomes increasingly important to bring the King into active participation in the game, and to the centre of activities. In order to prevent your opponent from doing this, it is often good play to use your Rook for this purpose alone. This may be done along a rank or a file, keeping the opposing King to the top or side of the board. This function of the Rook is often needed when Rook and pawn are left against Rook.

*Rook behind the Passed Pawn*

Very often, when you have an isolated passed pawn in a Rook and pawn ending, your opponent will use the offensive powers of his Rook to attack that passed pawn.

Now, often, your King is not in a position to defend that pawn, and the Rook must do it.

*To support a passed pawn, place the Rook behind it.*

If that pawn is supported by a Rook on the same rank as it stands, and is attacked by an opposing Rook on its file, it simply will not be able to move forward at all without being lost. Similarly, the supporting Rook will be unable to move and pave the way for supporting it on the next rank forward. So support on the rank is unsatisfactory. It is possible that the supporting Rook by playing on that rank may be able to fulfil one of its other main functions, in which case whether to play it there or behind the pawn must be decided on the relative merits of the two functions.

In diagram 145 White has a passed pawn on the third rank, and is supporting it with his Rook *behind*.

As the pawn moves up the board (clearly White's objective) so does the Rook's mobility increase until (diagram 146) it has control over almost the entire board. Eventually Black's Rook cannot move from where it stands without risk of the pawn being queened.

Supposing, however, the Rook was in front of the passed pawn?

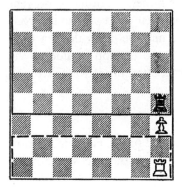

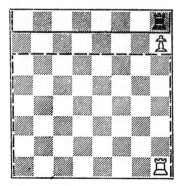

*Diagram* 145                    *Diagram* 146

In diagram 147 is an illustration of the Rook in front of the passed pawn. At the outset he controls the greater area of the board, as shown. But as the pawn advances so does he lose his advantage in "board control" and his difficulties increase.

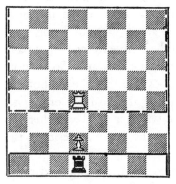

If the pawn should eventually reach the seventh rank it would be White's Rook that would be unable to move.

*When supporting or attacking a passed pawn with Rook, place the Rook behind the passed pawn.*

*Diagram* 147

The reader will have to use his judgment as to which of these three main functions he will put his Rook as, although the first and second are to some extent compatible, the Rook cannot be behind a passed pawn *and* on an open file at one and the same time! Speaking very generally, however, when there are many pawns remaining on the board, seize the most advantageous open file, and use the Rook offensively.

If your opponent has been able to get his Rook in an offensive position, look round for the possibilities of counter-attack with your own Rook. (He may leave the open file in going after a pawn.) Remember, *the Rook is an attacking piece.*

When one pawn only remains, what part must the Rook, and, of course, the King, play in trying to queen that pawn?

## ROOK, KING AND PAWN AGAINST ROOK AND KING

Can Rook, King and pawn win against Rook and King?

The first thing to note is that if the opposing King can reach the queening square of the pawn, then it is not possible to force a win against correct play. The same method of showing the mechanism whereby the pawn *can* be queened, will be used as in the case of King and pawn against King. What, then, is the ideal position in this case?

### The Ideal Position—Method One

The ideal position from which the pawn can be queened against the best possible defence is shown below (diagram 148).

There are, however, two distinct methods of winning the game from this position according to the line of defence adopted by the player with Rook and King only. Diagram 148 will be used to demonstrate Method One, and in this case White has the move.

Note the chief characteristics of this position. White's King in support of the pawn and on

*Diagram 148*

its queening square, and his Rook cutting off the approach of the black King (major function (2) ).

White plays—

$$1 \quad \text{R–B1 } ch$$

This drives the King farther away from the pawn, since after 1 ... K–K3; 2 K–K8, and Black simply cannot prevent the pawn from queening.

| 1 | ... | K–Kt3 |
|---|-----|-------|
| 2 | R–B4 | |

The Key move. Why it is essential for the Rook to go to the fourth rank will be seen shortly.

| 2 | ... | R–B8(a) |
|---|-----|---------|
| 3 | K–K7 | R–K8 ch |
| 4 | K–Q6 | R–Q8 ch |
| 5 | K–K6 | R–K8 ch |
| 6 | K–Q5 | R–Q8 ch |
| 7 | R–Q4 | |

and the pawn cannot be prevented from going in. (Now it can be seen that the Rook must be played on to the fourth rank, in order to be in position for interposing at this stage.)

(a) If Black had played here 2 ... K–Kt4, White plays—

| 3 | R–B7 | K–Kt3 |
|---|------|-------|
| 4 | R–K7 | |

followed by

| 5 | K–K8 | |
|---|------|---|

and the pawn must get in.

Note that it is of no avail for Black to try to stop this manœuvre by, say, 4 ... R–KR7, as then White replies 5 R–K8, the King comes out via B7, Kt6, B5, Kt4, etc., and when the checks can no longer be made, the pawn goes in protected by the Rook.

### The Ideal Position—Method Two

Supposing, however, it had been Black's move in the last position, and in order to prevent the line of play in Method One, he had played 1 ... R–QB5. Now we would have the position

*Diagram* 149

in diagram 149, with White to play, but unable to go on to the fourth rank with his Rook.

Method Two is accomplished as follows—

| | | |
|---|---|---|
| 1 | R–B1 *ch* | K–Kt3 |
| 2 | K–K7 | R–K5 *ch* |
| 3 | K–Q6 | R–Q5 *ch* |
| 4 | K–K6 | R–K5 *ch* |
| 5 | K–Q5 | R moves, say, R–K7 |
| 6 | R–Q1 | |

and now the pawn can move in.

### Arriving at the Ideal Position

It is, of course, not always possible to reach the ideal position. If the defending King can reach the queening square of the pawn, it is not possible to win. The first task then is to try to prevent that King from reaching its objective.

In the position that follows, White had been able to hold up the opposing King with his own, and the pawn has to be advanced from the fourth rank.

*Diagram 150*

White is to play, and the ideal position could be reached by the following line of play.

| 1 | R–Q6 | R–Q7 | (*a*) |
|---|------|------|-------|
| 2 | P–Q5 | R–Q8 | |

Black, having got his Rook *behind* the passed pawn is not going to relinquish that position to White.

| 3 | K–B7 | R–B8 *ch* (*b*) |
|---|------|-----------------|
| 4 | R–QB6 | R–Q8 |
| 5 | P–Q6 | K–K1    (*c*) |
| 6 | R–B2 | R–Q5 |
| 7 | R–K2 *ch* | K–KB2 |
| 8 | P–Q7 | R–QB5 *ch* |
| 9 | K–Q8 | |

arriving at the ideal position (Method Two).

(a) After 1 ... R–QR8 follows

|   |       |          |
|---|-------|----------|
| 2 | P–Q5  | R–R2 (ch) |
| 3 | K–B8  |          |

and the main possibilities are—

|   |            |          |
|---|------------|----------|
| 3 | ...        | R–R1 (ch) |
| 4 | K–Kt7      | R–K1     |
| 5 | K–B7       | R–K8     |
| 6 | R–Q8       | K–K2     |
| 7 | P–Q6 (ch)  | K–B2     |
| 8 | K–Q7 etc.  |          |

|   |            |          |
|---|------------|----------|
| 3 | ...        | K–K2     |
| 4 | R–K6 (ch)  | K–B2     |
| 5 | R–K1 etc.  |          |

|   |            |          |
|---|------------|----------|
| 3 | ...        | R–R8     |
| 4 | K–B7       | R–R2 (ch) |
| 5 | K–Kt6      | R–K2     |
| 6 | R–Q8       | R–K8     |
| 7 | K–B7 !     |          |

|   |            |          |
|---|------------|----------|
| 3 | ...        | R–R4     |
| 4 | K–B7       | R–R8     |
| 5 | R–K6       |          |

The above possibilities show how difficult these endings can be to win. For a more detailed study the reader is recommended to books devoted entirely to the endings. Simpler variations are shown in (b) and (c).

(b) If here Black plays 3 ... K–K2, White replies 4 R–K6 ch, K–B2; 5 K–Q6, R–Q7; 6 R–K1, R–Q6; 7 K–B6, R–B6 ch; 8 K–Q7, R–Q6; 9 P–Q6 and he can easily reach the ideal position.

(c) If here Black moves 5 ... K–K3, White replies 6 R–B2!!

R×P; 7 R–K2 *ch*, K–Q4; 8 R–Q2 *ch*, winning the Rook and the game.

What happens in this type of position when the pawn is on a Rook's file?

In the position in diagram 151, for instance, it depends entirely on who has the move, though this would not matter if Black's King were further away from the scene of action. In this position however, if White is to move, he wins as follows—

| | | | |
|---|---|---|---|
| 1 | R–B8 | | K–K2 |
| 2 | R–KKt8 | | R–KR7 |
| | | | (or anywhere on this rank) |
| 3 | K–Kt7 | | R–Kt7 *ch* |
| 4 | K–R6 | | R–R7 *ch* |
| 5 | K–Kt6 | | R–Kt7 *ch* |
| 6 | K–B5 | | |

and now we have the same position as in the ideal position (Method One, note (*a*) ). The white King simply marches up the board and Knight's and Bishop's files, and when the Rook can no longer check, the pawn goes in with the Rook as support.

But if it were Black's move, then with 1 ... K–K2 he prevents White playing R–B8, and thus he will have no means of forcing the black Rook off the Knight's file, and if the white Rook leaves the Bishop's file the black King can get there and prevent the white King's exit. The game would thus be drawn. So in the case of the Rook's pawn, the game cannot be won from the ideal position unless the opposing King is three files, or more, away from the pawn, with the stronger side to move.

*Drawing with Rook and King against Rook, King and Pawn*

Just as it requires correct play to win from the ideal position so does it require correct play to draw when the defending King has succeeded in reaching the queening square of the opposing pawn.

Let us examine a position where this has occurred.

*Diagram 152*

In the position shown in diagram 152, if White tries to drive Black's Rook off the third rank with his own Rook, Black exchanges with a drawn position, e.g.—

| 1 | R–KKt7 | R–QR3 |
|---|--------|-------|
| 2 | R–Kt6  | R × R |
| 3 | K × R  | K–K2  |
| 4 | K–B5   | K–B2  |

with the opposition.

Without the exchange of Rooks he draws as under—

| 1 | ...   | R–QR3  |
|---|-------|--------|
| 2 | P–K5  | R–QKt3 |
| 3 | R–R7  | R–QB3  |

The black Rook *must* remain on the *longer* side of the board, so as to have more space for manœuvring.

4    P–K6                    R–B8

The defending Rook remains on the third rank on the longer side of the board, until the opponent pushes the pawn on to that rank. The Rook then goes to its eighth rank.

5    K–B6                    R–B8 *ch*

Now the only way White can avoid the perpetual check is to bring his King down the board towards the Rook doing the checking. When he becomes three squares away from the pawn, however, Black immediately plays his Rook on to the pawn's file. White is then compelled to defend it with R–R6, and after Black's reply K–K2, poor passed pawn is lost!

*Conclusions*

When the aid of the King is required to queen the pawn the conduct of the ending should be based on the following observations.

(*a*) *In order to Win.* In order to win with Rook, King and pawn against Rook and King, the following conditions should be achieved—

(1) The ideal position should be reached. Normally this can be done when the opposing King can be cut off two files away from the pawn, and cannot reach the queening square.

(2) In the case of the passed pawn being a Rook's pawn, the opposing King should be cut off at least three files from the pawn and the attacker reach the ideal position *and* have the move.

(*b*) *In Order to Draw.* (1) The defending King must reach the queening square of the pawn.

(2) The defending Rook must keep to the third rank, and remain on the longer half of the board (the side with more space for manœuvre) and remain there until the pawn, supported by

the King, moves on to that rank. (Note that if the attacking Rook is on that rank, then he does not keep the King confined to its rank and the same technique could apply, as if the seventh rank were the queening one.)

(3) When the pawn moves on to the defender's third rank, the Rook must immediately be played to its eighth, and the perpetual check operations commenced.

ADVICE ON USE OF ROOK IN THE END-GAME

The following general rules should be observed, though naturally, very much depends on the position.

(1) Remember that *the Rook is essentially an attacking piece*. When there are many pawns left on the board, seize the open file, try to infiltrate into your opponent's position, and get him on the defensive.

(2) Remember that to support or attack a passed pawn with a Rook, place the Rook *behind* the passed pawn.

(3) Remember that as the number of pawns remaining on the board diminishes, so it becomes increasingly important to utilize the King as much as possible. Therefore try to bring your King into the battle, and try to cut off your opponent's, either with a Rook or your own King.

## THE QUEEN IN THE END-GAME

It may seem strange, but the Queen is not such a good end-game piece as the Rook! Do not get the idea from this that for some mysterious reason it is better to be left with a Rook against an opponent's Queen. However, if you have a material advantage when this stage of the game is reached, it is nearly always better that you and your opponent have a Rook each, than a Queen each.

Why this is so will be seen from the Queen's characteristics enumerated below—

(1) The Queen is extremely powerful in the end-game.

The open board with its long lines and diagonals give it great scope for its eight-direction movement, and square control. In addition it is the only piece besides the Rook that can mate with the help of the lone King.

(2) Its immense power is a disadvantage!

When both sides have a Queen left in the ending, the enormous strength of this piece tends to overshadow slight superiority in material. The advantage of a pawn, even two pawns, is often insufficient to win the game.

(3) Perpetual check.

The Queen on an open board is able in most cases to subject the rival King to a series of checks from which there is no escape or refuge.

This provides the side weaker in material with excellent opportunities for drawing the game by perpetual check. In order to win the game the stronger side may, therefore, continually be trying to exchange off that troublesome Queen for his own. It does not say much for the value of the Queen in the end-game when the side stronger in material is nearly always glad of the chance to change them off!

This "checking" factor is even more important when we recall two points in relation to the end-game.

(a) The Queen cannot mate without the help of its King.

Thus the weaker side is not unduly worried by attacks from the opposing Queen alone—he does not fear perpetual check!

(b) The King is required in the centre of activities. Whether this be for pawn support or to assist in trying to effect a mate, the nearer the King approaches to the scene of action the more exposed will it become to perpetual check from the opposing Queen, and a draw for the weaker side.

We can now understand why the difficulty of winning a Queen ending can often be insurmountable.

### EXCHANGE OF QUEENS

To win an ending when holding a material advantage, it is on many occasions essential to be able to exchange the Queens. Let us consider the case of a single pawn advantage as shown in diagram 153.

*Diagram 153*

*Diagram 154*

In this type of position sometimes the pawn and sometimes the King can be used to assist in this exchange. Here with White to play

| 1 | Q–Kt5 *ch* | K–R2 |
|---|-----------|------|
| 2 | Q–K7 *ch* | |

and the assistance of the pawn compels Black to exchange or lose his Queen.

In this next position, diagram 154, two points are shown. Firstly the use of the King in forcing the exchange, and secondly, a pitfall the weaker side must always guard against—careless checking.

From the above position, Black without thought might play

1 ...                     Q–K7 *ch*
2 Q–K4 *ch*

forcing the Queen exchange. With White to play this exchange could be forced on the first move.

The strong side must always make sure in cases where there is a single pawn advantage that after the exchange of Queens, his remaining pawn will be able to queen, otherwise the exchange is pointless.

### QUEEN AGAINST PAWN AT THE SEVENTH

The Queen has little difficulty in stopping the advance of a single pawn. It has only to get in front of the pawn when it cannot be dislodged, and the arrival of its own King will eliminate the support of the pawn's King.

The only case to be considered, therefore, is when the lone pawn supported by its King has reached the seventh rank, and the Queen has been unable to get to the queening square of the pawn.

There are four distinct possibilities into which an ending of Queen against pawn at the seventh rank may fall, namely

### The Queen Wins

(1) Queen can capture the pawn with the help of its King.

(2) Queen does not prevent the pawn from queening, but mates with the help of its King.

*Case* (1). *Queen can capture the pawn.* Here the Queen can capture the pawn with White to move by the following procedure. The Queen continually checks the defending King, approaching the pawn with each check. The King in order to stay in contact with the pawn it is defending is eventually obliged to occupy the queening square. This gives White a "free" move which is utilized to bring his own King towards the pawn. The procedure is repeated until the attacking King reaches the pawn when it can then be captured.

In the position illustrated in diagram 155, the initial checking moves of the white Queen are numbered, while the possible moves of the black King are marked with a cross. As can be seen it will eventually be forced on to the queening square, e.g.

*Diagram 155*

|   |           |        |
|---|-----------|--------|
| 1 | Q–Q5 *ch* | K–B7   |
| 2 | Q–K4 *ch* | K–Q7   |
| 3 | Q–Q4 *ch* | K–B7   |
| 4 | Q–K3      | K–Q8   |
| 5 | Q–Q3 *ch* |        |

and now the King must go to the queening square or the pawn is lost. So White plays

6  K–K6

By a repetition of this procedure it will be seen that the white King eventually reaches the third rank, and can assist in the capture of the pawn.

*Case* (2). *Queen does not prevent the pawn from queening, but mates.* This example, illustrated in diagram 156, is of great importance, as the pawn is a Bishop's pawn, which pawn is liable to allow a draw by stalemate as will be shown later.

White plays 1 K–B3! Note that he must not on any account play 1 K–K3, because of the reply 1 ... P–B8(Kt) check!

| 1 | K–B3 ! | P–B8(Q) *ch* |
|---|---|---|
| 2 | K–K3 ! | |

and whatever Black plays he is mated.

*Diagram 156*

### Drawn Game

*Case* (3). *Queen cannot prevent the pawn from queening.* In its purest form this case is extremely rare, but an example is given in diagram 157.

*Diagram 157*

*Diagram 158*

Here the white Queen has no checks available, so even with the move is unable to prevent the pawn from queening.

*Case* (4). *Queen cannot capture the pawn or a stalemate occurs.* This can occur in the case of a Bishop's pawn and a Rook's pawn. An example involving the Bishop's pawn is shown in diagram 158. In order to win by the method given in Case (1) White must play

| | | |
|---|---|---|
| 1 | Q–K5 *ch* | K–Q7 |
| 2 | Q–B4 *ch* | K–K7 |
| 3 | Q–K4 *ch* | K–Q7 |
| 4 | Q–B3 | K–K8 |
| 5 | Q–K3 *ch* | |

and the black King is forced to B8. The white King now approaches

| | | |
|---|---|---|
| 6 | K–Q5 | |

But this time the defending King emerges *on the Rook's file side of the pawn.*

| | | |
|---|---|---|
| 6 | ... | K–Kt7 |

Now must follow

| | | |
|---|---|---|
| 7 | Q–Kt5 *ch* | K–R7 |
| 8 | Q–B4 *ch* | K–Kt7 |
| 9 | Q–Kt4 *ch* | K–R7 |
| 10 | Q–B3 | K–Kt8 |
| 11 | Q–Kt3 *ch* | K–R8 *!* |

Instead of meekly retiring behind its pawn the black King abandons it, and White cannot capture because of the resultant stalemate, and in order to prevent the pawn from queening, White must not only move his Queen again, thus gaining no "free" move for the advance of his King, but must, in so moving, abandon the Knight's file (or allow the pawn to Queen) thus allowing Black's King to regain contact with the pawn.

An example of stalemate involving the Rook's pawn follows in diagram 159.

*Diagram 159*

Here, when the Queen has driven the King on to the queening square there is once more no free move to allow the white King's approach, since to retain control of the Knight's file causes stalemate.

Unless the attacking King happens to be already in contact with the pawn, a pawn on a Rook's file on the seventh rank supported by his own King can draw against the Queen.

### Queen and Pawn against Queen

As has already been learnt from its end-game characteristics, the advantage of a single pawn is hardly ever sufficient to win when the Queens are present. The weaker side can generally give endless checks, so the most likely chance of the stronger side to win is to change off the Queens. Without being able to do this there is still a chance of winning if the pawn has reached the seventh rank, though even then it is by no means always possible.

It will be remembered that in our table of values of the pieces, the Queen was considered equal to two Rooks. How then, does this assessment compare when there are few pieces remaining on the board?

### Queen against Two Rooks

In more cases than not a Queen is inferior to two Rooks in the end-game, though the advantage is by no means overwhelming, and can vary according to the position as do the values of all the pieces. There are two very distinct advantages held by the pair of Rooks.

(1) Two Rooks can mate without the help of the King.

The effect of this is to make the attack of two Rooks against the opposing King frequently more dangerous than that of the Queen against its opposing King.

(2) Two Rooks can often capture a pawn despite protection from both King and Queen.

Thus by giving up the two Rooks for the Queen a pawn may be gained as in this position.

Counting the two Rooks and Queen as even, the material shown in diagram 160 is equal. Now the black Queen's Knight's pawn cannot have more material to defend it so after 1 R × P *ch*, Q × R; 2 R × Q *ch*, K × R, White has gained a pawn, and

should win the game, as he has a protected passed pawn on the Knight's file, and a potential passed one on the King's Bishop's file.

These advantages are by no means always sufficient, as the Queen has at least the ever-recurring possibility of a per-petual check to avert loss of the game.

*Diagram 160*

The player with the Rooks must also be very careful to keep them supporting one another and acting as a pair, or else he may find that a long series of checks finally results in the loss of one of them!

## THE BISHOP AND KNIGHT IN THE END-GAME

The sharpness of the contrast between these two pieces serves to bring out with extra clarity the peculiar characteristics of each, when considered together.

In only one respect, are they similar. Unlike the Rook, neither a Bishop nor a Knight can, with the aid only of the King, give mate to the opposing King. This has two important bearings on end-game strategy.

(1) A single Rook left at the end means that the game can be won, whereas if a single Bishop or Knight is left, the game is only a draw.

(2) Thus, when both sides have one minor piece (Knight or Bishop) left, and there is also one pawn still on the board, the weaker side can, given the opportunity, always sacrifice his minor piece for the opponent's pawn, and thus secure the draw. This is rarely possible with Rook and pawn left against Rook.

## CHARACTERISTICS OF THE BISHOP AND KNIGHT

Their differences and distinctions, the points both for and against either piece are discussed under the headings below. In conclusion they will be summarized and tabulated for the convenience of the reader.

### (1) *Range and Speed*

The BISHOP has a long range of action, and can be as fast across the board as a Rook or Queen.

The KNIGHT has only a very short range, and is very slow across the board.

The Knight can be pursued across the board by the major pieces, and must even run very hard to escape the pursuit of the opposing King. The Bishop on the other hand seldom has the slightest difficulty in escaping from a challenge from a King, and indeed compares favourably with the Rook in ability to get about the board in the more open type of ending.

### (2) *Square Control*

The BISHOP has a maximum of thirteen squares against the Knight's control of eight.

The KNIGHT, however, can manœuvre so as to control both black and white squares according to what may be required of it, whereas the Bishop can control squares of *one colour only*.

Thus, in a Bishop and pawn ending, the Bishop is likely to suffer much reduced powers if the opposing pawns are on opposite coloured squares to those on which the Bishop is operating.

Some of this disadvantage is made up for by the larger *number* of squares the Bishop is likely to control.

### (3) *Attacking and Defensive Powers*

The BISHOP has one great advantage as a defensive piece. When it is defending a pawn, and is itself attacked, it can nearly always move, and *yet still protect the pawn*. A KNIGHT, on the other hand, if it is protecting a pawn and has to move, is bound to be defending that pawn no longer.

The KNIGHT, as an attacking piece, has greater capabilities than the BISHOP. Owing to its peculiar mode of movement, it is a specialist in the "forking" type of attack, with double and diverse threats. In addition, it can "attack without being attacked." In other words, if a Knight is attacking a piece, that piece is automatically never in a position to capture that Knight (unless, of course, it is another Knight!) The Knight, however, does not show up to great advantage when attacking mobile pawns. A pawn which, when attacked by a Knight, moves forward, often leaves the Knight with a considerable amount of manœuvring to do before it is again in a position to attack that pawn.

Against this, it must be remembered that when a Knight attacks an immobile pawn defended by a Bishop, that Bishop cannot drive the Knight away as it will be on a different coloured square.

### (4) *Two Bishops and Two Knights*

When we compare two Bishops with two Knights, the balance swings very much in favour of the Bishops. (Two

Bishops are a *pair* of Bishops, two Knights remain two single Knights.)

The Bishops combine beautifully together, the one doing everything the other cannot do. Both black and white squares are under their fire, they are speedy and all embracing in their functioning, and together (with help, naturally, from the King) can fairly easily force mate on a lone opposing King, which the two Knights cannot do.

It was mentioned earlier in the book that two Bishops are a strong weapon. With the more open board in the end-game that strength shows up to an even greater degree than early in the game.

The Knight, however, is essentially an individualist and does not combine readily or easily with other pieces, even with his fellow Knight. A Knight can defend another Knight (Bishops cannot protect one another) but only at the expense of *both* Knights remaining immobile.

It would have to be a very out of the ordinary end-game position where two Knights would be preferable to two Bishops.

### Special Circumstances Concerning Bishop and Knight

#### (a) Drawing Chances

(1) *Bishop and Rook's pawn.* Even a Bishop and pawn may be insufficient to win the game at the end, if that pawn is on a Rook's file.

If the queening square of the pawn is of the same colour as the squares on which the Bishop is operating, the game can easily be won. If, however, that square is of the opposite colour, and the defending King can reach the queening square of the pawn, the game is a draw.

In the position shown in diagram 161, for instance, the black

King moves to Kt2, and then cannot be driven away from the corner.

Here the Knight has the advantage since in all normal cases Knight and Rook's pawn can always win against the opposing King, as the Knight can man-œuvre so as to play on to the queening square.

(2) *Bishops of opposite colour.* The type of ending in which pawns and Bishops remain but the opposing Bishops are oper-ating on *opposite coloured squares* is of very great significance.

Diagram 161

When this occurs, the chances are heavily in favour of the game ending in a draw. Even the advantage of two pawns is frequently insufficient to give the stronger side a win, as for example in the position illustrated in diagram 162.

Diagram 162

Black has merely to mark time with his Bishop remaining always on the diagonal it now occupies, and White has no means of pushing on his pawns, without losing them. His Bishop, not operating on the white squares is useless, and consequently one might almost consider the game as a Black Bishop against two white pawns.

Thus you must endeavour to keep a Bishop of the same colour as your opponent's when at an advantage, and have one of opposite colour when at a disadvantage in the end-game. An example leaving an opponent with a "Bishop of the opposite colour" was given under "The Art of Exchanging," page 76, and would repay another perusal (diagram 102).

(3) *Sacrifice of a Bishop or a Knight for a pawn.* It has already been mentioned that a draw can be secured by a minor piece against a minor piece and one pawn, by giving up the minor piece for the pawn.

(4) *Bishop or Knight against King and pawn.* Either a Bishop or a Knight can stop a single pawn from queening, provided that they do not happen to be too far away to prevent it from running straight in, even when that pawn is supported by its own King and their King is too far away to be of any assistance.

For the BISHOP, this is all too simple, since as soon as the pawn attempts to cross its line of fire it is immediately "sacrificed" for the pawn, and it is far too swift for the King to have any chance of driving it away.

The KNIGHT can also prevent a pawn from queening unassisted, but not without difficulty, and careful play. As we know from its characteristics, its lack of speed means that the King can drive it away, but by utilizing its "forking" type of attack, even though driven away, it can still force a draw from the King and pawn.

The technique required is shown in diagram 163.

Here is what may be described as a typical position. The black King is too far away

*Diagram 163*

to be of any assistance to the Knight, which must alone prevent that pawn from winning for White.

Note that the Knight has been able to "catch" the pawn and is preventing it from queening without assistance from its King, but that King is well up in support.

White plays

|   | 1 K–K7 | Kt–K4 *!* |
|---|--------|-----------|

If

|   | 2 P–Q8(Q) | Kt–B3 *ch* |
|---|-----------|------------|

winning the Queen.

### (b) "Good" and "Bad" Bishops

When two opposing Bishops are operating on the same coloured squares in an end-game, the relative positions and potentialities of each Bishop are often the deciding factor of the game. A Bishop may be a "good" Bishop, which means that it has mobility and attacking possibilities— i.e. the opponent's pawns are mostly on the same coloured squares as the Bishop.

A "bad" Bishop would be one hemmed in and relatively immobile and with the opposing pawns on opposite coloured squares. (Note that if one side's pawns are on squares of one colour it is likely the opposing pawns will be on squares of the opposite colour.)

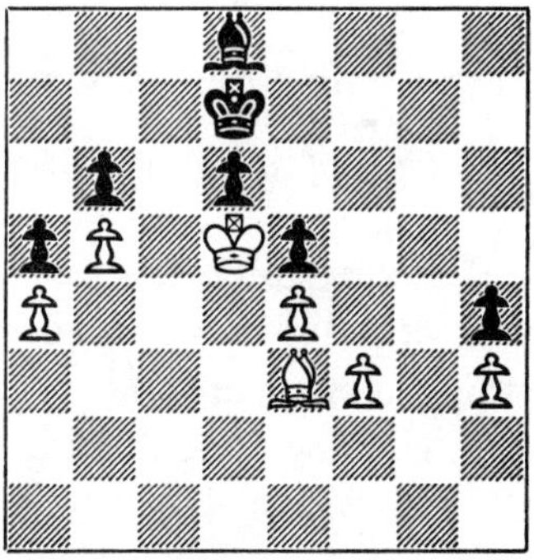

In diagram 164 for instance is an end-game where the material is equal but White has a "good" Bishop and Black a "bad" one. In spite of the equality in material White can win the game by play based on the following lines—

*Diagram 164*

|   |       |        |
|---|-------|--------|
| 1 | P–B4  | P×P    |
| 2 | B×P   | B–K2   |

The Queen's pawn is threatened.

|   |       |
|---|-------|
| 3 | B–K3  |

Now Black must defend his Knight's pawn either with Bishop or Knight.
So if

|   |       |        |
|---|-------|--------|
| 3 | ...   | B–Q1   |
| 4 | B–B2  |        |

A tempo-saving move.

|   |       |        |
|---|-------|--------|
| 4 | ...   | K–B2   |

(The Bishop cannot move.)

|   |       |         |
|---|-------|---------|
| 5 | K–K6  | B–Kt4   |
| 6 | B–K1  | B–Q1    |
| 7 | B–Q2  | *Resigns* |

(The Bishop cannot move.)

Play based on B–B2 would also win for White.

This very important potential difference in the values of the opposing Bishops in an ending should be remembered as the ending approaches, and every effort made to ensure that it is you who have the "good" Bishop!!

In the case of Knights, there does not exist the same differentiation, since Knights can attack both colours of squares. However, for a Knight to be "good," it must have strategic squares on to which it can play, and from which it cannot readily be driven off. If such squares are, or can be made, available, then a Knight may do more than hold its own against another Knight or a "bad" Bishop.

EXAMPLES OF ENDINGS FEATURING BISHOP AND KNIGHT

(1) *Knight defeats Bishop.* Examine the position in diagram 165. Black has a "bad" Bishop. It has little scope for movement and three of the White pawns are on squares of the opposite colour. On the other hand the Knight is well placed, and cannot be readily driven from its vantage point.

Diagram 165

Whichever side has the move, White can win. If it is Black's move, White has the opposition of the Kings. If White is to move he gains that opposition with the waiting move.

    1   P–Kt3

Now Black cannot move the Bishop without loss of a pawn, so must play

    1   ...                K–Kt3

The game might then proceed,

    2   K–K5               K–Kt4
    3   K–Q6

and White can win the Queen's Bishop's pawn, leaving him with a passed pawn.

(2) *Bishop defeats Knight.* In the following position (diagram 166) White again has a Knight and Black a Bishop, but this time, although the Knight appears reasonably well placed, the Bishop is a "good" Bishop.

Three of White's pawns are on black squares, and the Bishop has a good range of activity.

Black can win from this position by

|   |   |       |
|---|---|-------|
| I | ... | B–B7 |
| 2 | K–B3 |    |

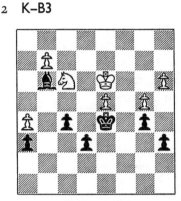

*Diagram 166*

The white Knight cannot move.

|   |   |       |
|---|---|-------|
| 2 | ... | K–K5 |
| 3 | Kt–Q2 *ch* | K–K6 |
| 4 | Kt–B3(*a*) | B–Kt6 |

and the black King cannot be prevented from capturing the white King's Knight's pawn. If

|   |   |       |
|---|---|-------|
| (*a*) 4 | Kt–B1 *ch* | K–K7 |
| 5 | Kt–R2 | B–Kt6 |

and once again the white King can capture the King's Knight's pawn.

(3) *Two Bishops versus Bishop and Knight.* It has been mentioned that owing to their co-ordination two Bishops are very often superior to Bishop or two Knights. An example showing how this superiority can occur is given on page 170.

The following table will assist the reader in summarizing the characteristics and relative merits of the Bishop and Knight in the end-game.

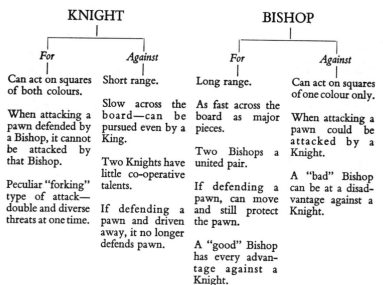

| KNIGHT | | BISHOP | |
|---|---|---|---|
| *For* | *Against* | *For* | *Against* |
| Can act on squares of both colours. | Short range. | Long range. | Can act on squares of one colour only. |
| When attacking a pawn defended by a Bishop, it cannot be attacked by that Bishop. | Slow across the board—can be pursued even by a King. | As fast across the board as major pieces. | When attacking a pawn could be attacked by a Knight. |
| | Two Knights have little co-operative talents. | Two Bishops a united pair. | A "bad" Bishop can be at a disadvantage against a Knight. |
| Peculiar "forking" type of attack—double and diverse threats at one time. | If defending a pawn and driven away, it no longer defends pawn. | If defending a pawn, can move and still protect the pawn. | |
| | | A "good" Bishop has every advantage against a Knight. | |

## EXAMPLES OF END-GAME PLAY

To embark upon a very detailed discussion of all the possible types of endings would be beyond the scope and intention of this book—indeed it would require a book of its own—so the authors have contented themselves with a selection of the more usual types taken from actual play.

### Transposition from Middle- to End-game

During the intense struggle of the middle-game, it very often happens that one or other of the players acquires a small advantage, either in position or material which, though too small to produce any decision in the middle, may be decisive in the ending.

For example, he may be a pawn up. Now with many pieces left on the board such an advantage is seldom felt, but if he can bring about an ending, especially with the Queens off the board, that pawn may bring victory.

*Diagram* 167

Take for instance the position shown in diagram 167.

Before reading on try to sum up this position, with Black to move.

Though still in the middle-game, Black sees that by reducing the pieces the ending will be in his favour as he will have the initiative and have White on the defensive. So he begins by exchanging the Queens.

| 1 | ... | Q × Q |
|---|-----|-------|
| 2 | R × Q | Kt × P |
| 3 | Kt × P | P × Kt |
| 4 | B × Kt | R–R5 |

Already Black is exerting pressure. The Bishop cannot move or a pawn will be lost, so White has to defend it with

| 5 | R–Kt1 | R–B1 |
|---|-------|------|

This Rook now attacks the pawn on the semi-open file, and White's other Rook must play a defensive role. Remember that the Rook is at its best in an attacking capacity—both Black's Rooks are now attacking while White's are defending.

| 6 | R(B1)–B1 | P × P |
|---|----------|-------|
| 7 | P × P | B–B1 |

This threatens to open up the Queen's Bishop's file with P–Kt4, the pawn being pinned on the file because of 8 P × P, R × R; 9 R × R, R × B.

| 8 | Kt–B3 | P–Kt4 |
|---|-------|-------|
| 9 | Kt–Q2 | B–R3 |

Black now threatens

|      | 10  ...  | R × B  |
|------|----------|--------|
|      | 11  R × R | B × Kt |

winning a piece.

Without proceeding further or going into any analysis, it can be seen that by forcing on the end-game Black has at least the initiative and indeed it is difficult to see how White can avoid the loss of at least a pawn.

### Appreciating the Situation in an End-game

It is essential to form a plan for conducting an ending. This is just as important as it is in the opening and the middle-game, and haphazard play at the end is the quickest way to lose from a winning or level position. The position illustrated in diagram 168 occurred in a match game.

Since White was to play in the actual game we will work on this assumption.

*Diagram* 168

### Summary

*White's Viewpoint.* The position of the white King is inferior to the black one, not being so centrally placed nor so far up the board.

The black Bishop is a "good" Bishop, having freedom of movement over the board. It is unobstructed by its own pawns which are nearly all on white squares, whereas the white pawns, being on black squares are nearly all liable to attack from it.

The white Knight, however, is not so well placed, being

decentralized and having few convenient squares to make for—the obvious one on Q4 would lead to disaster, since after the exchange by the Bishop the passed pawn would be lost.

In view of these factors, it appears that White should be well satisfied to draw the game.

Remembering our characteristics of the Knight and Bishop in the end-game, we know three important things applicable to this case.

(1) The Bishop alone cannot mate.

(2) Bishop and pawn cannot win if the pawn is a Rook's pawn, and the queening square is of a different colour to the squares on which the Bishop is operating, i.e. Black's Rook's pawn.

(3) The swiftly moving Bishop is of greatest advantage when there is play on both sides of the board.

Bearing these facts in mind we can base our plan to secure the draw on the following line of play.

(1) White should try to exchange off the black King's Knight's pawn leaving him with an isolated Rook's pawn. This might be accomplished by P–R3 and P–KKt4.

(2) Then if even for the two Queen's side pawns he can get rid of the black Queen's Knight's pawn play becomes confined to one side of the board, and the handicap of the slowness of the Knight is minimized.

(3) In addition, with these pawns gone, opportunity may easily occur to sacrifice the Knight for Black's King's pawn and King's Bishop's pawn (which, should be noted, are on white squares), when with only the Rook's pawn remaining he cannot win, as the opposing King can easily reach the queening square.

*Black's Viewpoint.* In assessing White's chances we have dealt, even if in a negative way, with most of Black's considerations. Undoubtedly Black has the superior game and his plan will therefore be directed to trying to win.

The first step should be to block up any discomforting advances by White on the King's side, which can be accomplished by Black playing P-R4. This leaves the initiative there entirely in Black's hands, since he can always advance P-KKt4.

Then advance with the King to the Queen's side, and endeavour to penetrate into the pawn position there. This penetration can be stopped only by the white King abandoning the King's side, or the posting of the Knight at Q2. In the latter case by retiring the Bishop to Q1 action on both sides of the board is possible, the dislodging of the Knight by B-Kt3 and P-K6, the advance of the King (after the Knight has had to move) either to K5 or B5, and also the advance of the King's Knight's pawn to Kt4.

Such diverse and numerous threats would cause continuous anxiety to White and from Black's viewpoint furnish the best chance of winning the game.

By examining all endings in this way, assessing the merits of the position, remembering the characteristics of the pieces taking part, deciding whether to try for a win, or be thankful to draw, you will at least be able to formulate a plan of action, and most probably a good plan too.

### King and Pawns against King and Pawns

The importance of knowing how to play endings with only King and pawns remaining on the board cannot be over-emphasized, since there is the possibility that every ending may eventually be reduced to this stage.

Two examples are given of this type.

The appended position (diagram 169) is simple to assess. Though there is pawn equality, Black's Queen's side pawns can produce a passed pawn whereas White's King's side majority cannot. Black should therefore win. It is only a matter of technique, but it is this technique that should be thoroughly understood.

From a general point of view, Black's advantage lies in the fact that his King has only one task to perform, that of holding

*Diagram 169*

the central pawns—preventing the capture of his Queen's pawn and stopping the white King's pawn from queening. This can be done by playing to K3. His single pawn on the King's side can hold up both White's King's side pawns.

On the other hand White's King has two tasks to perform— to hold the centre and also to stop Black's Queen's side passed pawn, if and when created, from queening. Now we know from the slowness of the King in moving about the board that this is no easy task.

Another important factor, as always in this type of ending, is the question of tempos. Let us assume that Black plays 1 ... K–K3, White must play K–Q4 to hold the centre. *Now if those pawns alone were on the board,* whoever has to move would lose his pawn as he must leave it. Black would, therefore, *not* play K–K3 but K–K2. Now if White played 2 K–Q4, K–K3 and now White must lose his pawn, so in fact White would play K–K3, and neither side would dare approach the pawns!

However, with the other pawns, as in the actual position, Black could compel the white King to leave the central pawn by creating a passed pawn on the Queen's side and threatening to queen it.

This, therefore, will be the technique employed to try and win this ending.

| 1 ... | K–K3 |
| 2 K–Q4 | P–Kt4 |

advancing the unopposed pawn.

| 3 P–R3 | P–QR4 |
| 4 P–KR4 | P–R4 |

There is no object in Black's allowing his opponent too many spare tempos, as would result if White was able to play P–KR5 P–(KR3)–4. Such tempos may be invaluable.

| 5 P–R3 | P–Kt5 |
| 6 P–R4 | P–Kt6 |
| 7 K–B3 | K × P |

Black has achieved his first object.

| 8 K × P | K–Q5 |

The winning move. Black is able, as he had foreseen, to reach the "ideal" position for queening the pawn.

| 9 K–B2 | K–K6 |
| 10 K–Q1 | K–Q6 |
| 11 *Resigns* | |

To show the importance of correct application of the principles we have learnt, it is very useful to note a method of Black's play which would *not* have produced a win.

| 1 ... | K–K3 |
| 2 K–Q4 | P–Kt4 |
| 3 P–R3 | P–QR4 |
| 4 P–KR4 | P–Kt5? |

This move presses blindly on with the plan, but allows White the valuable tempos mentioned after move 3 in the winning variation.

|   |       |        |
|---|-------|--------|
| 5 | P×P   | P×P    |
| 6 | P–R5  | P–Kt6? |

There was still time to save a tempo by P–R3

|    |       |      |
|----|-------|------|
| 7  | K–B3  | K×P  |
| 8  | K×P   | K–Q5 |
| 9  | K–B2  | K–K6 |
| 10 | K–Q1  | K–Q6 |

Now Black has what would be the ideal position, but White has a larger number of tempos in hand.

|    |       |
|----|-------|
| 11 | P–R6  |

Now we know that the only way to queen is to force the white King to move away from the opposition. With only Kings and pawns on the board this is done by

|    |      |       |
|----|------|-------|
| 11 | ...  | P–Q5  |

But after this move in this position, White merely plays

|    |       |
|----|-------|
| 12 | P–R4  |

and the ideal position is lost and Black is to move. If

|    |              |            |
|----|--------------|------------|
| 12 | ...          | K–K6 (or B6) |
| 13 | K–K1 (or B1) | P–Q6       |
| 14 | K–Q1         | P–Q7       |
| 15 | P–R5         |            |

Since the remaining black pawn would be a Rook's pawn, it is also useless to give up the Queen's pawn for the two white Rook's pawns. The game would be drawn.

### Rook and Pawns against Rook and Pawns

Endings involving Rooks and pawns are perhaps the most frequently occurring types, and thus the example which follows (diagram 170) will be dealt with in great detail.

The white King is well in the centre of the Queen's side players. It has a greater choice of movement than the black, which is tied down to defence against the opposing Queen's pawn. In its defensive role, however, the black King is better

placed, as it can help in stopping White's passed Queen's pawn from queening, whereas the white King is well away from Black's passed King's Bishop's pawn.

*Diagram 170*

White has a supported passed Queen's pawn on the sixth rank, but this is offset by Black's passed King's Bishop's pawn, which although only on the fourth rank can easily be supported by the Knight's pawn and, as has been pointed out, requires the white Rook to stop it.

White's Rook is behind his passed pawn which is a good place and fulfils one of its functions, but the black Rook attacks White's isolated King's Rook's pawn *on the file*, thus immobilizing it, and exerts pressure on White's fourth rank, thus to a certain extent restricting White's King.

With Black to play, he plans to make use of these considerations in this way. First, block up any white advances on the Queen's side, and second, advance his passed pawn on the King's side, thus making the "centre of gravity" there. He plays

I ...                    P–QKt3

Now if White does nothing here, Black wins a pawn.

2  P×P                   P×P

If 2 P–Q7 *ch* for White 2 ... K–Q1 and his Queen's pawn would certainly be lost sooner, or later.

| 3 | K–Kt4 | K–Q2 |
|---|-------|------|
| 4 | R–KKt2 | |

White tries to transform his Rook into an attacking one.

| 4 | ... | R–R2 |
|---|-----|------|
| 5 | R–Kt6 | |

White's idea is to be able to play P–B5, which will give him either a passed Rook's pawn or else enable him to support his Queen's pawn with the King, but now Black puts the second half of his plan into operation.

| 5 | ... | P–B5 |
|---|-----|------|
| 6 | P–B5 | P–B6 |
| 7 | R–Kt1 | |

The poor position of the white King in defence is now seen, and unfortunately for White the attractive looking 7 R–Kt3 will not work, e.g. 7 R–Kt3, P–B7; 8 R–*KB3*, R–R5 *ch*! and the King must go to the third rank after which Black plays R–R6, pinning the Rook!! (R×R, P–B8(Q) ).

| 7 | ... | P×P *ch* |
|----|--------|----------|
| 8 | K×P | P–B7 |
| 9 | R–KB1 | R×P |
| 10 | P–R4 | P–Kt4 |
| 11 | P–R5 | P–Kt5 |
| 12 | P–R6 | P–Kt6 |
| 13 | P–R7 | R–R1 |
| 14 | K–Kt6 | P–Kt7 |
| 15 | *Resigns* | |

*Two Rooks against Two Rooks*

Here again, though there is also a Bishop on either side, the main theme is as above.

Examine the position in diagram 171. The material is even,

and with Bishops of opposite colours, a draw would seem to be indicated. If we recall the characteristics of the Rooks, it will be

*Diagram 171*

remembered that their great strength lies in their combined efforts supporting one another's actions.

With Black to play, he begins with

| 1 | ... | B–B6 |
| 2 | R–K3 | B–Kt5 |
| 3 | P–B3 | P–QB3 |
| 4 | R–KKt5 | B–B4 |

If 4 R–Q1, B×RP; 5 R×P, B–B2; 6 Rook moves B×P gaining a pawn.

| 5 | R–Q3 | K–Kt2 |

Black plays a far-sighted move based on the factor mentioned above. He sees that by sacrificing the pawn at Q3 he will be able to separate the two white Rooks from one another for some time, and expects to gain an advantage, which will be greater than the loss of the pawn, by having the use of his own two Rooks combining together.

| 6 | P–QKt4 | B–R2 |
| 7 | R×P | B–K6 |

This is the key move, of what is actually a sacrificial combination.

8   R–KKt4

Note that R–Kt3 is not possible because of B–B5.

8   ...              P–KR4

Note also the point of 5 ..., K–Kt2, since, if the King were on Kt1, this would be met by R×P *ch*.

9   R–R4              B–Kt4
10   R–R3

This Rook is now cut off from his companion.

10   ...              B–B5
11   R–Q3              R–QB1

Black now aims to break up White's pawn chain, by attacking it at its centre.

12   P–Kt3              B–Kt1
13   R–Q2              P–QB4
14   B–Q5              P×P
15   P×P              R–B8 *ch*
16   K–K2              R–QKt8

attacking the pawn from behind.

17   P–Kt4              P×P
18   P×P              R×P

At least Black has regained his pawn!

19   R–B2              B–B2
20   R–B5              R–Kt7 *ch*
21   K–Q3              R–Q2
22   K–B4              B–K4

This threatens White with the loss of his Rook after R–B7 *ch*. And if 23 K–Q3, R–QKt6 *ch* winning the other Rook.

23    R–QKt3

the "lost" Rook returns to the fray, but alas! he arrives too late.

| 23 | ... | R–B7 *ch* |
|----|------|-----------|
| 24 | K–Kt4 | B–Q3 |
| 25 | R–B3 | B × R *ch* |
| 26 | *Resigns* | |

Apart from the technical aspects, there is at least one important thing to be learnt from this excellent ending. In an apparently even position Black conceived a plan. This plan was based primarily on a knowledge of the functions and characteristics of the various pieces in the end-game; in this particular instance, that two Rooks acting together as a team are stronger than two separate Rooks. He even had the courage to sacrifice material in order to bring this knowledge to reality without necessarily knowing, in absolute detail, the method whereby he would ultimately gain the advantage.

Knowledge, backed by the courage to use it!

*Bishop against Bishop of the Same Colour*

Endings involving Bishop against Bishop occur very often. We know that when the opposing Bishops are moving on squares of a different colour there is an overwhelming tendency

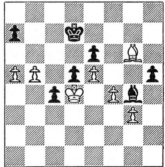

*Diagram 172*

to a draw. From this it follows that the greatest interest lies where there are what are always known as "Bishops of the same colour."

White is to play (diagram 172).

*Appreciation of the Situation*

(a) *Position of the Kings.* The white King is better positioned than the black. It is in the centre of the board, in this case also in the centre of activity, besides being two squares farther up the board than its opposing number.

(b) *Pawn Situation.* Black has two supported passed pawns. They are, however, held up by the well-placed White King standing on a square from which it cannot be dislodged by the opposing Bishop. In addition, the only one of these able to move, the Bishop's pawn, has a queening square of the opposite colour to its Bishop.

White has no actual passed pawns, but has two potential ones, the Queen's Knight's pawn and either the King's pawn or King's Bishop's pawn. Though on that balance alone Black might be considered to have the better pawns, there are two other factors to counter-balance this score. Firstly, if, and when, White has actual passed pawns, they will be two *distant* passed pawns, whereas Black's are two *united* passed pawns which are already held up by the opposing King.

The reader will recall that very often the distant passed pawns are at an advantage in these cases. Secondly, the white pawns are nearly all on squares different from the opposing Bishop's, while the opposite applies to Black's pawns.

(c) *Relative Merits of the Bishops.* White's Bishop has a greater mobility and, as just mentioned, can attack the black pawns. Black's Bishop has not quite the same degree of mobility, and cannot attack the opposing pawns at the moment. It is, therefore, less effective than White's. From this appreciation of the respective positions, we must reach the conclusion that White has the advantage. How can that advantage be realized?

Clearly, to win the game the potential passed pawns must be made into actual ones. On the Queen's side this can be done by an immediate P–Kt6. But it is also clear that, if that alone is done, the black King can catch and capture that pawn with P×P and K–B2 or B3. So in order to cause real difficulties the other passed pawn must also be created. This can be done since by advancing P–B5 Black must capture or P–B6 follows and, if the Bishop captures, the pawn at K5 is passed after B×B, P×B. So White plays

| 1 | P–KB5 | P×P |

This is wisest, since the distant passed pawns will be more dangerous with no Bishop for Black to use.

| 2 | P–Kt6 | P×P |
| 3 | P–R6 ! | |

Though we have awarded this move an exclamation, it is the only logical way to carry on. White is aiming to win by means of the distant passed pawns. As we know, the farther apart they are, the more difficult are they to stop. This move, however, has an additional merit as well. It makes the queening square of the pawn the same colour as the Bishop, a most important factor as we know.

| 3 | ... | P–B6 |

The weight of the distant passed pawns is already felt. The black King cannot cope with both (e.g. K–B2; 4 P–K6, K–Q3; 5 P–R7) so Black is compelled to sacrifice both his passed pawns to open up the diagonal QR1–R8 for the Bishop.

| 4 | K×BP | P–Q5 *ch* |
| 5 | K×P | K–B2 |

An immediate B–B6 would be followed by 6 B×P *ch* and B–K4 cutting off the black Bishop from the diagonal.

| 6 | P–K6 | B–B6 |
| 7 | B×BP | *Resigns* |

Nothing can prevent the Black Bishop from being driven off the vital diagonal by B–K4, and thus White from queening one or other of the passed pawns.

This is a most instructive ending showing how White's plan for winning based on the strength of two distant passed pawns, and the restricted nature of Black's Bishop, succeeds admirably.

### Two Bishops against Bishop and Knight

Though there is also a Rook present on either side, the position

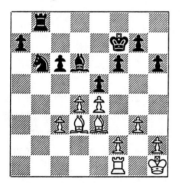

*Diagram* 173

which follows has as its main theme the pair of Bishops in action against Bishop and Knight.

White to play (diagram 173).

Assessing the position we see that Black has a distant passed pawn, and a better placing of his King. White has a pair of Bishops and an attacking Rook against the defensive one of Black's.

Believing that these advantages outweigh Black's, he tries to win by exploiting them.

|   |          |       |
|---|----------|-------|
| 1 | R–R1     | R–Kt2 |

Note more clearly now the attacking and defensive Rooks.

|   |          |       |
|---|----------|-------|
| 2 | P–KB4    | P×BP  |
| 3 | P×P      |       |

Against Black's distant passed pawn, which is now immobilizing the Rook in its defence, note the excellent central pawn formation of White's—a tower of strength—in contrast to Black's two isolated pawns.

|   |          |       |
|---|----------|-------|
| 3 | ...      | K–K1  |
| 4 | P–B4     |       |

This not only threatens P–QB5, but just look at the terrifying strength of this pawn formation, all supported by the Bishops. As we know from our study of pawn formations, this is the strongest possible formation of four pawns "structurally" and being absolutely centrally placed is also the strongest "functionally."

|   | 4 ... | Kt–Q2 |
|---|---|---|

The Knight retires in almost undignified haste, before the formidable array!

| 5 | P–K5 | B–Kt5 |
|---|---|---|

The Bishop must also leave the centre.

| 6 | B–K4 | R–B2 |
|---|---|---|
| 7 | P–K6 | Kt–Kt1 |

The Knight must move again and goes back to relieve the overburdened Rook of one of its defensive duties.

| 8 | P–KB5 | P–QR4 |
|---|---|---|
| 9 | B–B4 | R–B1 |

White could now win a pawn by B×Kt, but here we have an excellent example of how restraint is necessary in the endgame. By winning this pawn White would give up one of the main factors which influenced him into regarding his game as better—the pair of Bishops, and in addition would be left with Bishops of opposite colour, that potent drawing factor.

| 10 | B–B3 *!* |
|---|---|

He now threatens the combined moves of P–B5, B–R5 *ch* and B–Q6.

| 10 | ... | Kt–R3 |
|---|---|---|
| 11 | B–R5 *ch* | K–K2 |
| 12 | P–B5 | |

This shuts out Black's Bishop from the active part of the board.

|    | 12 ... | Kt×P |
|----|--------|------|

This sacrifice may well be said to be forced, since after B–Q6 *ch*, the white King's pawn can be run in and Black loses the exchange at least.

| 13 | P×Kt | B×P |
|----|------|-----|
| 14 | R–Q1 |     |

The attacking Rook threatens to help run the pawn in, despite Black's sacrifice.

|    | 14 ... | R–Q1 |
|----|--------|------|

The only way to prevent this.

| 15 | R×R  | K×R     |
|----|------|---------|
| 16 | B–B3 | *Resigns* |

The Bishop's pawn is lost and the passed Rook's pawn cannot get beyond R6. White's faith in the power of the two Bishops has been justified.

# CHAPTER V

# The Theory in Action

THE sections which follow contain a selection of games which illustrate the principles taught in this book.

The reader is asked to bear in mind that this alone is the object of the games which have been selected for this section and the comments which are made on them.

At the beginning of each game a summary is given, firstly of the higher strategy governing the general conduct of the game, and then of the minor strategical concepts utilized by either side in furtherance, or against that higher strategy. For the sake of brevity this summary appears under the headings "Higher Strategy" and "Weapons Employed."

It is suggested that before starting to play through each game the reader refer back to the chapters in which the concepts mentioned in the summary to the game are described, to refresh his memory.

Finally, the indulgence of the reader is asked in his judgment of the games themselves. At any single point there may well be what appears to be a "better" move than the one played. We should like the reader, however, to judge the moves made not on the idea that "If White plays this, Black could play that," but rather, "Is the move in accordance with the principles of opening development?" or, "Does that move further the higher strategy he has decided upon?"—that should be the criterion of whether a move is "good" or "bad."

## IN WHICH LACK OF DEVELOPMENT PAYS THE FULL PENALTY

When one player has completed his development, it will be

remembered that an assessment of the position would probably reveal one of three possibilities.

(1) Opponent not developed.

(2) Opponent developed, but weak centrally.

(3) Opponent developed and "equal" centrally.

The advice given in the first of these cases was, "Attack with pieces." The first game in this chapter gives an example of this being carried out.

## GAME No. 1

*Higher Strategy*

Correct central development.
Attacking with pieces against an undeveloped opponent.

*Weapons Used*

Pinning.
The threat of a discovered check.
Open and semi-open file.
Weakness of doubled isolated pawns.

|   | *White* | *Black* |
|---|---------|---------|
| 1 | P–K4    | P–K4    |
| 2 | B–B4    | B–B4    |
| 3 | P–QB3   |         |

Is this move in accordance with opening principles? Yes, because it is played as preliminary to P–Q4, a combination of moves which would counter the pressure Black has put on the central square at White's Q4.

|   | *White* | *Black* |
|---|---------|---------|
| 3 | ...     | Kt–QB3  |
| 4 | Kt–B3   | Kt–B3   |
| 5 | P–Q4    |         |

Here we have the move of which White's P–QB3 was the preliminary, and with it White attempts to gain command of his Q4, and thus improve his position in the all-important centre.

5 ...          P×P
6 P–K5          Q–K2

What is the reader's opinion of this move?

Firstly, it loses a tempo, since with the developing move of O–O the pin on the pawn is removed. Secondly, it looks very much like a case of utilizing the Queen too early in the game.

7 O–O          KKt–Kt1

The reply 7 ... Kt×KP would be very dangerous for Black as the Knight and/or the Queen could be pinned against the King after White's R–K1.

8 P×P          B–Kt3

The position after Black's eighth move is shown in diagram 174.

*Diagram 174*

Note the grip which White has already acquired on the centre of the board.

9 P–Q5          Q–B4

Once again at this early stage Black violates opening principles.

by using his Queen and bringing it out into the centre of activities.

10　Kt–R3　　　　Kt–Q5

White, however, finds a move with which he can continue his development, and also protect the Bishop.

11　B–K3

White continues with developing moves, and this pin compels the exchange of Knights, thus forcing the ill-placed Queen to retire and gaining yet another tempo.

11　...　　　　Kt × Kt *ch*
12　Q × Kt　　　Q–B1

After her unproductive excursion, the Queen returns ignominiously to base!

13　B × B　　　　RP × B (Diagram 175)

*Diagram 175*

For White the opening phase of the game is over. He is fully developed and castled, so let us assess the position. There can be no doubt into which of the three categories this falls! Black has not got a single (remaining) piece developed. The strategy needed is thus "attack with pieces and win." Let us see how he carries this out.

| 14 | Kt–Kt5 | K–Q1 |
| 15 | QR–B1 | |

Note that he places the Rook on the semi-open file.

| 15 | ... | P–Q3 |

He must somehow try to get his pieces into action. It is, of course, for the very reason that the King is so helpless without the support of his pieces that an attack against him is so effective in this category of game.

| 16 | P × P | P × P |

The semi-open file is fully opened.

| 17 | Q–K3 | |

Black's doubled and isolated pawns are very weak, and thus prove an object of attack. There is one important lesson to be learnt here though. This doubled pawn formation is attacked not because it is such a formation, but because its weakness affords another possible avenue of approach in the attack against Black's position. In any game, but particularly in this type, one must not lose sight of the overall strategy behind the conduct of the game. In this case it calls for an all-out attack with one's pieces. To waste time in attacking a doubled pawn formation, merely because it is a weakness, would allow the opponent time to bring out his pieces, and perhaps defend what was previously a hopeless position. Bigger things are in the offing for White than a mere pawn as will shortly be seen.

| 17 | ... | R–R3 |
| 18 | Kt–B7 | Q–K2 |

18 ... K × Kt would lose at least the Rook because of the discovered check.

| 19 | Kt–K6 *ch* | P × Kt |
| 20 | B × R | B–Q2 |

If Black takes the Bishop he would lose the Queen after
21 Q×P *ch*, K–K1; 22 R×B *ch*, K–B2; 23 R–B7.

| | | |
|---|---|---|
| 21 | **B–Kt5** | **K–K1** |

Again B×B loses the Queen.

| | | |
|---|---|---|
| 22 | **P×P** | **Kt–B3** |
| 23 | **R–B8** *ch* | *Resigns* |

The Bishop is pinned and the game is lost.

Black's lack of development rendered him powerless against
the onslaught of the white pieces.

### Open Games

The game just shown above is an excellent example of what
is known as an Open Game. Before passing on to the next
game it will be of great advantage to pause for a while and
consider what characteristics go to make up an open game.

First of all, what is an open game?

*Definition.* An Open Position is one in which—

(*a*) There are clear files, ranks, and diagonals, so that the pieces
have freedom to manoeuvre and attack.

(*b*) The pawn position is such that clear files, ranks and
diagonals can readily be produced by movement of these pawns.

The first thing the reader will notice is that the word "Position" has been used instead of "Game." Although "Open
Game" is a common chess expression, the principle under discussion at the moment is an "Open Position." A game may have
an open position right from the outset, but it equally might
have an open position only in its closing stages.

Having arrived at our definition, let us consider its implications.

(*a*) In the type of position where there are many open files,
ranks, and diagonals so that the pieces have ample space for

manœuvre and attack it follows, clearly, that it is of vital importance to have your pieces ready for immediate action. Thus in the type of game we have just seen, where the position tends to be open right from the start, *speed* of development is the keynote of success.

Already by move 9 the position is open, so White's 10 Kt–R3 is guided by this knowledge of the importance of speedy development. Rather than lose time by moving the already developed Bishop, he brings another piece into play to defend it, even though the Knight itself might possibly be better placed on B3. As he had probably foreseen that it would go into the attack at Kt5, even this is questionable.

(*b*) In this type of position, where the game can readily be "opened up" by movement, and most likely exchange of pawns, it is again of very great importance to have one's pieces ready for action, and thus develop quickly if the game tends this way early on. Otherwise, one's opponent will do so, and having got all his pieces ready for action, open up the game and attack!

Since the player better developed has the advantage in the open positions, the player whose pieces are not ready for action should try to prevent the position becoming open. Conversely, the player with a distinct advantage in development does his best to open up the game.

So the strategy against an undeveloped opponent "Attack with pieces" must be preceded, unless the position is already an open one, by "Open up the position" which will allow the full power of movement of the developed pieces and provide an access for those pieces into the opponent's position.

And now that the reader has learnt these characteristics of the open position, we would recommend him to play over once again the game we have shown, noting how White on moves 16 and 19 uses pawn moves to open up the position at Black's end of the board.

GAME No. 2

*Higher Strategy*

Dealing with an attack launched before development is complete.

Aggressive defence.

*Weapons Used*

Open files and diagonals.
Pinning.
Exchanging.

| | White | Black |
|---|---|---|
| 1 | P–Q4 | Kt–KB3 |
| 2 | P–QB4 | P–K4 |

This move strikes at the centre of the board, and as such is in accordance with the principles of opening. It is also played with the knowledge that if the pawn is captured, as happens in this game, then the resultant position tends to become an open one.

| | | |
|---|---|---|
| 3 | P×P | Kt–Kt5 |
| 4 | P–K4 | |

White plays a developing move, and does not try to defend the pawn. Such an attempt would allow the initiative to pass into Black's hands and, if an open position then resulted, Black's superior development might prove decisive.

| | | |
|---|---|---|
| 4 | ... | Kt×P |
| 5 | P–B4 | Kt–Kt3 |
| 6 | B–K3 | B–Kt5 *ch* |
| 7 | Kt–Q2 | |

Note the harmony of development that White decided upon on move 6. Foreseeing the Bishop's check he brought out his own Bishop first, thus allowing 7 Kt–Q2. To answer the check with Kt–B3 would allow Black the option of exchanging and creating doubled isolated pawns.

| 7 | . . . | Q–K2 |
|---|---|---|
| 8 | Q–B2 | Kt–B3 |
| 9 | B–Q3 | Kt–R5 (Diagram 176) |

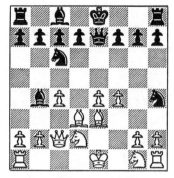

*Diagram* 176

Black starts an attack which is certainly a dangerous one, but he does it before completing his development. White's strategy is, therefore, to beat it off, knowing that if he does so, Black's lack of development will cause trouble when a counter-attack is launched.

| 10 | K–B2 | B–B4 |
|---|---|---|
| 11 | R–K1 | P–KKt4 *!* |

Having decided to attack on the wing, this move certainly furthers his plan. If White takes the pawn, the game is opened up still more.

| 12 | P–B5 |
|---|---|

Though he has no disadvantage in development, White avoids opening up the game. As the defender, his interest is to keep closed all possible lines by which the opposing pieces can approach his position.

| 12 | . . . | Kt–K4 |
|---|---|---|
| 13 | Q–B3 | Kt–Kt5 *ch* |
| 14 | K–B1 | O–O |

Against his adopted strategy! The Rook was in a position to join the attackers, now it is locked away.

15   P–B6 !

White seizes his opportunity and begins a method of blocking the path of Black's attacking pieces and, at the same time, opening lines for his own counter-attack.

| 15 | ... | Kt × B *ch* |
|----|-----|-------------|
| 16 | R × Kt | Q–Q3 |
| 17 | P–K5 | Q–K3 |
| 18 | R–Kt3 | P–KR3 |
| 19 | KKt–B3 | Kt–B4 |
| 20 | Kt × P ! | |

With this sacrifice, White completes his development and opens up the game for all his pieces. Having thus an open game and full mobility for his pieces, White extracts the penalty for Black's failure to complete his development.

| 20 | ... | Kt × R *ch* |
|----|-----|-------------|
| 21 | P × Kt | Q–Kt5 |

Naturally Black cannot take the Knight, as loss of his Queen would follow B–R7 *ch*.

| 22 | QKt–B3 | P–Q3 |
|----|--------|------|
| 23 | B–R7 *ch* | K–R1 |
| 24 | R × P | Q × KtP |
| 25 | Q–B2 | |

Prevents mate and threatens mate!

| 25 | ... | Q–B7 *ch* |
|----|-----|-----------|
| 26 | Q × Q | B × Q |
| 27 | K × B | B–K3 |
| 28 | Kt × B | P × Kt |
| 29 | B–B5 *dis. ch* | K–Kt1 |
| 30 | B × P *ch* | *Resigns* |

Mate is unavoidable. (30 ... R–B2; 31 Kt–Kt5, R–KB1; 32 R–Kt6 *ch*, K–R1; 33 B×R, R×B; 34 Kt×R *ch* and 35 R–Kt7.)

A premature attack, tempting though it seemed, pays the penalty of ultimate defeat!

## IN WHICH THE CENTRE IS IGNORED

The second possibility that might occur when one has completed one's development, is that of the opponent's being developed but weak centrally.

In the game that follows Black concentrates on speed of development alone and ignores the position in the centre. This allows White to do two things. To establish a great superiority in the centre, and to block up Black's position. Black's advantage in development thus becomes both temporary and useless— temporary because his cramped position makes it extremely difficult for him to complete it, and useless because his closed position does not allow the already developed pieces room for manœuvre and attack.

White's grip on the centre virtually strangles his opponent who can only free himself at the cost of a piece and the game. White uses his control of the centre to launch an attack on the King's wing. Not having control of the centre, Black is unable to get his pieces across the board to the defence of that wing.

GAME NO. 3

*Higher Strategy*

Utilizing an opponent's haphazard development to gain command of the centre.

Using that command of the centre to launch a wing attack.

*Weapons Employed*

Backward pawn.

Creation of weaknesses in opponent's pawn structure.

Open files.
Knight outpost.
The art of exchanging.

| | White | Black |
|---|---|---|
| 1 | P–K4 | P–QB4 |
| 2 | P–Q4 | P×P |

This exchange is justifiable, being towards and not away from the centre.

3    Kt–KB3

To take the pawn with the Queen would lose a tempo (Kt–QB3).

3    ...          P–K3

Note that the pawn *could* be defended by P–K4 (if 4 Kt×KP, Q–R4 *ch*), but to try to keep the pawn permanently would take up all Black's energies which should at this stage be devoted to development.

| | | |
|---|---|---|
| 4 | Kt×P | B–B4 |
| 5 | Kt–Kt3 | B–Kt3 |
| 6 | Kt–B3 | Kt–K2 |
| 7 | B–KB4 | O–O |

(diagram 177)

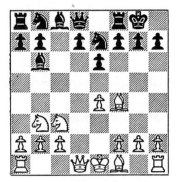

*Diagram* 177

Black hastens on with his development, but disregards the position in the centre.

His Queen's pawn is at present a potential "backward pawn," which if blockaded would not only give White a great superiority in the centre, particularly in space, but would make it extremely difficult for Black to develop his Queen's Bishop.

### 8 B–Q6

White places the Bishop there, and the Queen's pawn has become backward and blocked.

### 8 ... P–KB4?

This move plays straight into White's hands, enabling him to support the blockading Bishop with a pawn which can no longer be attacked by another pawn.

| 9 | P–K5 | P–QR3 |
| 10 | B–K2 | QKt–B3 |
| 11 | O–O | R–B2 |

This developmental stage has now been completed, at least for White. Let us, therefore, assess the position. Black is developed certainly except for his Queen's Bishop which is securely shut in. He is, however, weak in the centre of the board where it is difficult to see how he can progress, and the gain in space White has acquired gives his pieces greater mobility.

In addition Black has a central backward pawn at his Q2. In this position it is not so much the inherent weakness of the pawn that matters, but that its backwardness gives Black a very cramped game, hampering the completion of his development. How then, shall White proceed?

An all-out attack with pieces, as in Game No. 1, would hardly be likely to succeed here. Black has probably enough pieces in action to defeat it. The next possibility to consider is an attack in the centre. Now, although White has a definite superiority there, his superiority is based on the restricted state of the black forces and, in opening up lines for the penetration of his own pieces, would most likely also release Black's for defensive action. So White decides on an attack on the King's wing, which will present his opponent with the problem of trying to bring his cramped pieces over to that side in defence.

Before embarking on this he realizes that he must prevent all possibility of a black counter-attack in the centre, and to do this his immediate object consists of consolidating his hold on that centre.

12   K–R1

With this he releases the Bishop's pawn to add to the protection of the King's pawn.

12   ...          P–B5?

This certainly prevents the intended P–B4, but releases hold on the central K5 square, which White immediately occupies.

13   Kt–K4          Kt–B4<br>
14   B–R5

What is the object of this move? Black's Rook is so tied up by the two Bishops that P–Kt3 is forced. This sets up a further weakness in Black's pawn structure, and by releasing his grip on his KB3 provides an "outpost" for the Knight, if, and when, White should wish to use it. An excellent example of creating pawn-weaknesses in an opponent's position.

14   ...          P–Kt3<br>
15   B–KKt4          Kt–Kt2<br>
16   Q–B3          P–KR4<br>
17   B–KR3          Q–R5

Black brings his only other immediately available piece to the defence of his King's side.

18   Kt–B6 ch

The Knight outpost is occupied.

| 18 | ... | K–R1 |
| 19 | Q–K4 | Q–Kt4 |
| 20 | P–Kt3 | |

If 20 ... P×P; 21 BP×P and White as the attacker has succeeded in opening up another file.

| 20 | ... | P–B6 |

Black does not wish to open up.

| 21 | Kt–Q2 ! | B–Q1 |

For Black to take this Knight would be fatal for him.

| 22 | Kt(Q2)×P | Q–R3 |
| 23 | R–KKt1 | B×Kt |
| 24 | P×B | Kt–K1 |
| 25 | B–B4 | Kt×P |

Desperation! Black's position is unenviable. If ... Q–R2, 26 Kt–Kt5. If ... Q–B1, 26 Q×KtP.

Rather than move his Queen he therefore attacks White's. But White has the move and this advantage is used by exchanging in the right sequence to win a piece.

| 27 | Q×Kt | Q×B |

If he takes the Queen, then White takes his and he is a piece down. He is compelled by a check to do so next move, however.

| 28 | Q×B ch | R×Q |
| 29 | P×Q | R×P |

Quite rightly he seizes the seventh rank, but it provides insufficient compensation for the lost piece, and White's continued attack on the King's wing eventually forces a mate.

| 30 | QR–QB1 | R×BP |
| 31 | R–B8 ch | Kt–Kt1 |
| 32 | Kt–K5 | R–Kt2 |

| 33 | Kt × P *ch* | K–R2 |
| 34 | Kt–B8 *ch* | K–R3 |
| 35 | Kt × QP | R × Kt |
| 36 | QR × Kt | |

White has now doubled Rooks on what as far as the Black King is concerned is the equivalent of the seventh rank.

| 36 | ... | R × BP |
| 37 | B × P | R–K2 |

and now White mates in four moves. It might be of interest to the reader to complete the mate!

## IN WHICH ATTACKS IN THE CENTRE BREAK THROUGH

We have now seen examples of games in which the conduct of the opening has been at fault in the case of one of the players. The third of our categories, not yet discussed, is that in which both sides are developed, and neither has any marked central advantage.

In these cases the reader will remember that there are two main possibilities for continuing the game.

(1) Attack in the centre.

(2) Attack on a wing.

We know that other things being equal, an attack in the centre, if it can be successfully accomplished, is likely to be more telling than one on the wing.

In the first of the games shown here, though both sides have approximately equal central control at the conclusion of their development, Black makes a move which adds to White's power in that most important part of the board. As a result White sees a way of attacking, which breaks through the centre and leads to a won game.

In the second game manœuvring for position follows development, and results in White's breaking through on one wing while Black succeeds in a similar break-through in the centre. The centre one proves more dangerous and Black wins.

GAME NO. 4

*Higher Strategy*

An attack in the centre.

*Weapons Used*

A hidden pin.
An open file.
A pair of Bishops.
Opening up the game when attacking.

| | White | Black |
|---|---|---|
| 1 | P–K4 | P–QB4 |
| 2 | Kt–KB3 | P–K3 |
| 3 | B–K2 | Kt–QB3 |
| 4 | P–Q4 | P×P |
| 5 | Kt×P | P–Q3 |

Note that Black is not running any risks of being burdened with a backward Queen's pawn as occurred in Game No. 3.

| | | |
|---|---|---|
| 6 | P–QB4 | P–QR3 |
| 7 | Kt–QB3 | Kt–B3 |
| 8 | O–O | Q–B2 |
| 9 | P–QKt3 | B–K2 |
| 10 | B–B3 | B–Q2 |

White's move increased the pressure on Q5.

| | | |
|---|---|---|
| 11 | B–Kt2 | O–O |

The opening phase is over. Note that both sides are developed completely, in accordance with the principles, and while White has gained a little in central space, Black's position looks immune from the possibility of a break-through there.

12    R–K1                    Kt × Kt?

Has the reader any objections to this move?

It is true that it exchanges one of White's "centre" pieces, but it brings his Queen into the centre of the board to take its place, and has thus increased White's strength there relative to Black's.

13    Q × Kt                  B–B3
14    QR–B1                   KR–Q1

White now sees that there are two *hidden pins* which may possibly be exploited to achieve a break-through in the centre.

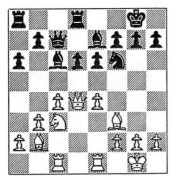

*Diagram 178*

Before proceeding we suggest that the reader examines this position to see them for himself (diagram 178).

The first hidden pin to note is on the black Knight. If White's Knight were not on the diagonal QR1–KR8 then the opposing Knight would be pinned because of the mate threat with Queen and Bishop.

Strictly speaking it is not fully pinned even then, as it could move to K1, but at least it could not move elsewhere.

The second pin would occur if neither the Knight nor the Queen's Bishop's pawn of White's were on the Queen's Bishop's file when the Bishop would be pinned against the black Queen.

Having noted these potential pins, White sees a method

whereby he can launch an attack on Black's apparently impregnable centre.

15    Kt–Q5 !

Knight cannot take Knight because of one pin. If the Knight is not taken, the black Queen must move and, in order to save the Bishop, must go to Q2, after which White can at least win an exchange by Kt–Kt6. If 15 ... B×Kt; 16 BP×B, and White has at least gained control of an important open file, and is in a position to advance in the centre if he wishes.

| 15 | ... | P×Kt |
|----|------|------|
| 16 | BP×P | Q–Q2 |
| 17 | P×B | P×P |
| 18 | P–K5 | |

This move provides another excellent example of an attacker opening up the game to provide lines of attack for his pieces.

| 18 | ... | P×P |
|----|-----|-----|
| 19 | Q×P | |

Note the powerful scope of White's two Bishops on the long open diagonals.

| 19 | ... | B–Q3 |
|----|--------|-------|
| 20 | Q–KKt5 | P–KR3 |
| 21 | Q–R4 | QR–B1 |
| 22 | B×Kt | P×B |
| 23 | Q×RP | B–B1 |
| 24 | Q×BP | B–Kt2 |
| 25 | Q–Kt5 | Q–Q7 ? |

This move seems to regain Black a pawn, or at least establish a Rook on the seventh rank, but alas! poor Black!

26    R–K8 *ch !*          *Resigns*

If he takes the Rook the black Queen is lost. If 26 ... K–R2; 27 B–K4 *ch* and mate next move.

GAME No. 5

*Higher Strategy*

Central advance as opposed to opponent's wing advance.

*Weapons Used*

Pin on a diagonal.
Exchanging.
Open file.
Mobile pawns.

|   | *White* | *Black* |
|---|---------|---------|
| 1 | P–K4 | P–QB4 |
| 2 | Kt–KB3 | P–Q3 |
| 3 | P–Q4 | P×P |
| 4 | Kt×P | Kt–KB3 |
| 5 | Kt–QB3 | P–KKt3 |
| 6 | B–K2 | B–Kt2 |
| 7 | O–O | O–O |
| 8 | B–K3 | Kt–B3 |
| 9 | R–Kt1 (diagram 179) | |

*Diagram 179*

White is now fully developed, but his last move was not directed towards strengthening his power in the centre. Black whose only undeveloped piece is, however, ready for instant movement, seizes the chance to equal his position in the centre.

| | | |
|---|---|---|
| 9 | ... | P–Q4 |
| 10 | Kt×Kt | P×Kt |
| 11 | P–K5 | Kt–Q2 |
| 12 | P–B4 | P–K3 |
| 13 | Kt–R4 | Q–R4 |
| 14 | P–B3 | R–Q1 |
| 15 | P–QKt4 | Q–B2 |

White's advance on the Queen's wing is justifiable, since at the moment Black cannot answer it with a centre counter-attack.

| | | |
|---|---|---|
| 16 | Q–Q2 | B–B1 |

This move is a preliminary to P–QB4 which would free Black's somewhat cramped position.

| | | |
|---|---|---|
| 17 | B–Q4 | P–QB4 |
| 18 | B–B2 | |

For White to exchange pawns and/or pieces would only assist Black in his objective of freeing his game.

| | | |
|---|---|---|
| 18 | ... | R–Kt1 |
| 19 | B–R4 | R–K1 |
| 20 | KR–B1 | B–KR3 |

The object of this pin will be seen next move.

| | | |
|---|---|---|
| 21 | Kt×P | Q×P ! |

Black gains White's advanced central pawn instead of the more obvious Kt×Kt and Q×P *ch.*

The reader will note that throughout this game Black concentrates with commendable judgment on the centre of the board. White certainly does not ignore the centre of the board, but does not fight so strongly over it as his opponent.

| | | |
|---|---|---|
| 22 | Kt×Kt | B×Kt |
| 23 | B–Kt3 | Q–Q3 |

Preparing for the advance of his King's pawn.

| | | |
|---|---|---|
| 24 | P–B4 | P–K4 |
| 25 | B–B3 | |

Clearly not Q×P or else 25 ... Q×Q; 26 P×Q, P×P.

| | | |
|---|---|---|
| 25 | ... | P–K5 |
| 26 | P–QB5 | |

As we have remarked above, Black has concentrated on bringing about a central advance. White, not so keen on that all important part of the board, now answers with an advance on the wing.

From now on this game furnishes an excellent example of the superiority of the central activities.

| | | |
|---|---|---|
| 26 | ... | Q–KB3 |
| 27 | B–K2 | P–Q5 |
| 28 | Q–Kt2 | QR–Q1 |
| 29 | P–Kt5 | B×BP |
| 30 | B×B | Q×B |
| 31 | P–B6 | B–B1 |
| 32 | B–B4 | Q–K6 _ch_ |
| 33 | K–R1 | K–Kt2 |
| 34 | R–KB1 | P–B4 |
| 35 | P–QR4 | Q–QB6 |

This offer of exchange of Queens is made for the purpose of opening up the central Queen's file for his Rook and further advancing his central pawns. White is almost forced to accept.

| | | |
|---|---|---|
| 36 | Q×Q | P×Q |
| 37 | QR–B1 | P–K6 |
| 38 | R×QBP | P–K7 |
| 39 | R–K1 | R–Q8 |
| 40 | R(B3)–B1 | R×R(B1) |
| 41 | _Resigns_ | |

The centre wins!

## IN WHICH THE CENTRE IS HELD FIRM AND
## A WING ATTACK BREAKS THROUGH

If it is not possible to carry out an attack in the centre, the next thing to consider is one on a wing.

Before doing so care should be taken to ensure that the opponent cannot counter with a central advance which, as we know, is likely to prove more dangerous than the original one on the wing.

In the following game the centre becomes locked, and White is able to conduct a successful wing attack.

GAME NO. 6

*Higher Strategy*
Locked centre. Wing attack.

*Weapons Used*
Harmony of development, leading to gain in space.
Pressure on a semi-open file.
Pawns as an attacking force.
Full preparation before final attack.

| | White | Black |
|---|---|---|
| 1 | Kt–KB3 | Kt–KB3 |
| 2 | P–QB4 | P–K3 |
| 3 | P–KKt3 | P–Q4 |
| 4 | P–QKt3 | B–K2 |
| 5 | B–QKt2 | O–O |
| 6 | B–Kt2 | P–B3 |
| 7 | O–O | QKt–Q2 |
| 8 | P–Q3 | Q–B2 |

Both players are fighting for Black's K4 square.

| | | |
|---|---|---|
| 9 | Kt–B3 | R–Q1 |

In view of the way in which Black's Queen's Bishop is

hemmed in, perhaps the more harmonious development would have been achieved by P–QKt3 and B–Kt2.

10   **Q–B2**          **Kt–Kt3**

This is a decentralizing move, taking away pressure from his K4 and restricting the movement powers of the Knight.

11   **P–K4**          **P–Q5**
12   **Kt–K2**         **P–K4**

White has now completed his development. Let us assess the

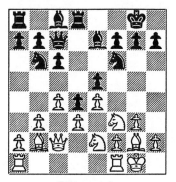

*Diagram* 180

position (diagram 180).

Owing to the last few pawn manœuvres, the centre has become locked. Any attempt at break-through there would afford very great difficulties to either player. Thus the question of an attack on a wing arises. Who has the best chances of launching a wing attack? White is more harmoniously developed than his opponent, who has a misplaced Knight at Kt3 and, not having yet moved his Queen's Bishop, his Queen's Rook is temporarily hemmed in.

Now of the two wing attacks we know that other things being equal an attack on the King's side is likely to be the more dangerous if it breaks through, as a mate threat may well be the outcome.

In this case, since Black has the majority of pieces on the Queen's side, a King's side attack by White is liable to be of even greater moment, since Black will be faced with the task of getting those pieces over to the attacked side.

White, therefore, decides to attack on the King's wing. The next question is—How can this be achieved?

One good way would be to advance the King's Bishop's pawn,

thus having the Rook supporting the attack as well. White decides to begin the attack in this way.

13　P–KR3

Why this move? It is a wise preliminary to the plan, otherwise after his P–KB4 Black would be able to move his King's Knight via Kt5 to the outpost at K6 which will be created by the White manœuvres.

13　...　　B–K3
14　Kt–Kt5　　P–B4

He anticipates White's pawn advance and adds protection to his Queen's pawn.

15　P–B4　　Kt–R4
16　Kt×B　　P×Kt
17　B–B1　　R–KB1

This move is the decisive error. He should have played P×P after which there would have been little difficulty in holding up White's attack.

18　P–B5

Note that all White's attacking pawns, King's Bishop's pawn, King's Knight's pawn and King's Rook's pawn, are mobile. The reader is asked to keep his eye on these pawns throughout the attack and notice that White always plays so as to *keep* them mobile.

18　...　　Kt–B1

This misplaced Knight begins his long and wearying journey to the rescue of the threatened wing! However, Black plays well in not taking the pawn now, as it would open up the diagonal for the opposing Bishop and release K4 for White to occupy either with the Knight or the Bishop.

19　P–KKt4　　Kt–B3

| 20 | Kt–Kt3 | Kt–Q3 |
|----|--------|-------|
| 21 | Q–K2   |       |

Both the Queen and the Knight have now crossed to join the attackers.

| 21 | ... | Q–B1 |
|----|-----|------|
| 22 | B–Q2 |     |

This connects the Rooks and enables them both to join in the attack if, and when, required. Note again throughout the attack how White does not try to press home until all his forces are ready.

The exercise of restraint when attacking is one of the most valuable assets a player can have, and one of the most difficult to acquire. The point is that an attack is generally most likely to succeed when all the pieces are well positioned to co-operate in it. The temptation is always to press home the attack *quickly* without waiting to get every piece into position first.

| 22 | ... | P–QR4 |

A belated attempt to attack on the opposite wing, which is soon frustrated.

| 23 | P–QR4 | P–QKt3 |

The position on the Queen's side is now locked.

| 24 | R–B2 | Kt–B2 |

With this move it becomes dangerous for White to delay his attack any longer, as Black threatens to set up a very strong defensive formation with P–KR3, Kt–R2 and Q–Q1 which would make it very difficult for the attack to continue.

| 25 | P–Kt5 | Kt–K1 |
|----|-------|-------|
| 26 | Q–R5  | Kt–R1 |
| 27 | Q–Kt4 |       |

Now that the black forces have been driven back, room is made for the King's Rook's pawn to join the attack.

| 27 | ... | P–Kt3 |
| 28 | QR–KB1 | |

Note that White still keeps his pawns mobile and does not play P–B6.

| 28 | ... | Kt–QB2 |
| 29 | P–R4 | Q–K1 |
| 30 | P–R5 | B–Q3 |
| 31 | B–R3 | Q–K2 |
| 32 | R–R2 | R–B2 |
| 33 | Q–R4 | KtP × BP |

Black has defended well, and not assisted his opponent by opening up the position, but now he is forced to do so.

| 34 | P × P | K–B1 |

The King prepares for flight!

| 35 | P–B6 | Q–Q2 |
| 36 | Kt–K4 | K–K1 |
| 37 | R–Kt2 | K–Q1 |
| 38 | P–Kt6 | P × P |
| 39 | P × P | Kt × P |
| 40 | R × Kt | Kt–K1 |
| 41 | Kt–Kt5 | *Resigns* |

## CLOSE GAMES

Under "Examples of End-game Play," we discussed the meaning and implications of an open position. The time has come to discuss the Close Position.

*Definition.* A CLOSE POSITION is one in which—

(*a*) There are few or no clear lines and the pieces have limited manoeuvring space and cannot directly attack.

(*b*) The pawn position is such that the position cannot readily be opened up by movement of the pawns, and where the only opening up would be by sacrifice of pieces.

To compare and contrast open and close positions study the two positions shown below.

The basic difference between these two positions is evident almost at a glance. Nevertheless, they are worthy of closer

(A)          Game No. 1                    (B)          Game No. 6
    (*after Black's 12th move*)                  (*after Black's 12th move*)

Diagram 181                              Diagram 182

study, and a consideration as to how they illustrate the definitions.

For the purpose of calculation below, a clear line has been considered as one having at least four squares in succession unoccupied by pawns.

On this reckoning position (A) has 8 clear files and 10 diagonals: total 18.

Position (B) has 1 clear file and 4 clear diagonals: total 5.

A similar type of check on the mobility of the pieces would show White's mobility as under—

|             | (A) |                          |             |     | (B) |                          |
|-------------|-----|--------------------------|-------------|-----|-----|--------------------------|
| Queen       | 10 possible squares to move. |    |     |     | 5 possible squares to move. |  |
| Rooks       | 6   | ,, | ,, | ,,              |             |     | 6   | ,, | ,, | ,,        |
| Bishops     | 12  | ,, | ,, | ,,              |             |     | 2   | ,, | ,, | ,,        |
| Knights (1) | 3   | ,, | ,, | ,,              | (2)         |     | 4   | ,, | ,, | ,,        |
| Total       | 33  | ,, | ,, | ,,              |             |     | 17  | ,, | ,, | ,,        |

So there can be no doubt that the two diagrams shown conform with the definitions of open and close positions.

With regard to the question of opening up close positions by sacrifice of pieces, examine (B) again. We can see that no movement of the pawns could readily open that position, but it could be opened by sacrifice of a piece or pieces. For example, as White has the move, he might play 13 Kt×KP! and after 13 ... Q×Kt; 14 P–KB4, followed by B or Kt×KP.

Thus the two black pawns which are locking the centre would be gone and the position readily opened up. However, it is more the exception than the rule that the advantage to be gained from opening the game outweighs the loss of material involved by the sacrifice.

From this discussion we can draw the following conclusions.

In a game which tends to be close from the outset, since the pieces have restricted mobility and an immediate attack is unlikely, the *speed* of development is not of such vital importance as in the open game. This does not mean that the pieces need not be developed, but that the factor of greatest importance is to get them into the best possible positions, even if it requires more than one developmental move to do so.

Thus in close games there is often time to post one or both Bishops at Kt2, though P–Kt3 must be played first. Similarly, in certain types of close positions the Queen's Knight may be best developed to K3 via Q2 and B1 even though this operation takes three moves.

Conversely, sheer speed of development may prove of no particular advantage, since an immediate attack against the opponent's position with pieces is usually difficult to achieve.

Thus we see the essential difference between open and close positions. In open positions the pieces have great manœuvrability, so they must be ready for instant action. In close positions their movement is restricted, so that the choice of *where* they are placed is of great importance—they cannot readily nip off to another part of the board! A rapid development without regard to the best position for each one may find the pieces "all dressed up and nowhere to go!"

Before leaving the subject of open and close games, there is one more point of interest. Since White has the first move, he should always be able to obtain a slight lead in development. It would thus seem that his interests are best served by an open type of game. Black, on the other hand, may well prefer to keep the game close at least in the very early stages. Hence, we see why so often when White opens the game with P–K4 Black answers, not with P–K4, which tends towards an open position, but with P–K3, P–QB4 or other moves which make it difficult to force open the game.

In view of this, White will often be content with a close game, opening, say, with P–Q4, and use his "first move" advantage to try and keep the initiative and a little extra pressure on his opponent's position.

## IN WHICH A WING ATTACK IS FRUSTRATED BY A COUNTER-ATTACK IN THE CENTRE

The last game showed a Wing attack where the centre was locked, thus preventing any chance of a counter-attack there. However, we know that if such a counter-attack is possible it may well be the most effective method against a wing attack. The game which follows gives an example of this happening.

GAME NO. 7

*Higher Strategy*

Wing attack met by counter-attack in the centre.

*Weapons Used*

Distant control of the centre.
Pinning.
A pair of Bishops against Bishop and Knight.

Open files with active Rooks.
A threat to occupy the seventh rank.

| | White | Black |
|---|---|---|
| 1 | P–QB4 | P–K4 |
| 2 | Kt–QB3 | Kt–QB3 |
| 3 | Kt–B3 | P–Q3 |
| 4 | P–Q3 | B–K3 |
| 5 | P–KKt3 | Kt–B3 |
| 6 | B–Kt2 | P–KR3 |
| 7 | O–O | Q–Q2 |

The reader will note that this has developed into a close game.
With this move Black threatens B–R6 forcing the exchange
of White's well-placed Bishop.

      8  R–K1

Now if 8 ... B–R6; 9 B–R1 !

| 8 | ... | B–K2 |
|---|---|---|
| 9 | P–QR3 | P–KKt4 (diagram 183) |

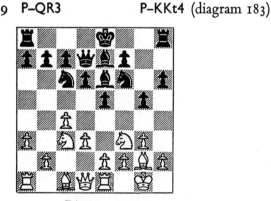

*Diagram* 183

Black, having completed his development, except for castling,
shows his hand. He has decided on launching an attack on the
King's side. White has a number of choices. To counter-attack

in the centre, or on the opposite wing, or to try and hold up the advance on the King's wing.

Since a counter-attack in the centre would be very difficult at the moment, he decided to conduct a preliminary attack on the opposite wing.

| | | |
|---|---|---|
| 10 | P–QKt4 | B–R6 |
| 11 | B–R1 | QR–Q1 |
| 12 | P–Kt5 | |

This move drives the black Knight away from the centre. Black would only strengthen White's position by playing Kt–Q5, e.g. 13 P–K3, Kt×Kt; 14 Q×Kt.

| | | |
|---|---|---|
| 12 | ... | Kt–Kt1 |
| 13 | B–QKt2 | Q–Kt5 |

White is now in a position to carry out a central counter-attack. How is this to be done? One way would be to play P–K3 followed by P–Q4. The disadvantage of this method would be that it would allow Black time to carry on his wing attack by P–KR4–R5.

White, therefore, decides that his Queen's pawn advance must be done with the support of the Queen on K3 instead of the pawn. This has the great advantage that with the Queen on the diagonal QB1–KR6, Black cannot immediately advance the King's Rook's pawn as he would lose the King's Knight's pawn.

| | | |
|---|---|---|
| 14 | Q–Q2 | QKt–Q2 |
| 15 | Q–K3 | P–Kt3 |
| 16 | P–Q4 | P×P |
| 17 | Kt×P | Kt–K4 |
| 18 | Kt–B6 | Kt×Kt |
| 19 | B×Kt *ch* | K–B1 |
| 20 | Q–Q3 | P–KR4 |
| 21 | Kt–Q5 | |

This move not only reveals the latent pin on Black's Knight, but simultaneously puts pressure on it.

| 21 | ... | R–R3 |
| 22 | P–B3 | Q–B1 |
| 23 | Kt×B | K×Kt |
| 24 | Q–K3 *ch* | |

White's central attack has broken through and is causing Black considerable embarrassment. This superiority in the centre in the now open position gives White opportunities in all directions.

| 24 | ... | B–K3 |
| 25 | Q×KKtP | R(Q1)–R1 |
| 26 | Q–R4 | Q–KKt1 |

White has now an excellent position, owing to the superior mobility of his pieces in an open position. How can this be exploited?

Since his Rooks are better positioned than Black's, their usefulness would be more telling if he could open up another file for them to operate on.

| 27 | P–K4 | Q–Kt3 |
| 28 | P–K5 | P×P |
| 29 | B×P | K–Q1 |
| 30 | B–Kt7 | |

Black is trying to get his King away to the comparative safety of the Queen's side. This move puts a stop to this.

| 30 | ... | R–Kt1 |
| 31 | QR–Q1 *ch* | K–K1 |
| 32 | B×P | |

The effectiveness of the pair of Bishops on open diagonals is again noticeable in this game.

| 32 | ... | K–B1 |
| 33 | B–Q6 *ch* | K–Kt2 |

| 34 | B–B4 | R(R3)–R1 |
| 35 | R × B | |

This sacrifice opens up the seventh rank for the benefit of the other Rook.

| 35 | ... | P × R |
| 36 | B–K4 | Q–K1 (*not* Kt × B!) |
| 37 | B–K5 | R–R3 |
| 38 | Q–Kt5 *ch* | R–Kt3 |
| 39 | B × R | Q × B |
| 40 | B × Kt *ch* | K–B2 |
| 41 | R–Q7 *ch* | K–B1 |
| 42 | Q–B4 | *Resigns* |

## *IN WHICH A WING ATTACK IS COUNTERED BY AN ATTACK ON THE OPPOSITE WING*

In the last game, we saw a wing attack dealt with by counter play in the centre. Naturally this cannot always be done. The next game shows an attack on the Queen's wing by White. This attack is facilitated by Black's somewhat doubtful opening play, which gives his opponent superiority in the centre and thus eliminates the possibility of a counter-attack there. The attack demolishes Black's Queen's side and his position becomes "hopeless."

He is left with only one resource. White's play has drawn the majority of his forces over to one side of the board, leaving his King's side only lightly guarded. Black throws all his resources into an attack on this opposite wing and pulls the "lost" game out of the fire.

GAME No. 8

*Higher Strategy*

Attack on one wing countered by attack on the opposite one.

*Weapons Used*

Breaking up of a pawn-chain.
Open files and diagonals.
Combined action of Rooks.
Knight outposts.

|   | White | Black |
|---|-------|-------|
| 1 | P–Q4 | P–Q4 |
| 2 | P–QB4 | P–K3 |
| 3 | Kt–QB3 | P–QB3 |
| 4 | Kt–B3 | P×P |

This move takes away pressure from Black's central K5 square and enables White to improve his position there with P–K4.

|   | | |
|---|---|---|
| 5 | P–K4 | P–QKt4 |

The attempt to hold the pawn he has won is very dangerous for Black, as the supporting pawn on his QKt4 is itself liable to attack from White's Queen's Rook's pawn. The reader should note the restraint exercised by White in attacking this pawn. He sticks to the principles by first developing then improving his position in the centre, thus preventing any counter there, and only then does he attack this pawn.

|   | | |
|---|---|---|
| 6 | B–K2 | Kt–Q2 |
| 7 | O–O | B–Kt2 |
| 8 | P–Q5 | Kt–B4 |
| 9 | P×BP | |

This removes one of the supports for the Queen's Knight's pawn.

|   | | |
|---|---|---|
| 9 | ... | B×P |
| 10 | Kt–Q4 | Q–Q2 |
| 11 | Kt×B | Q×Kt |
| 12 | P–QR4 | |

Two supports for the pawn having gone, only now does the attack come.

|    |         |                        |
|----|---------|------------------------|
| 12 | ...     | R–Q1                   |
| 13 | P×P *!* | Q–Kt2                  |
| 14 | Q–B2    | Kt–Kt6                 |
| 15 | R–R6    | Kt–KB3                 |
| 16 | B–K3    | B–B4 (diagram 184)     |

*Diagram* 184

An assessment of the position at this stage leaves no doubt as to which player stands better. Black's attempt to hold the gambit pawn has resulted in his being subjected to a fierce Queen's side attack, which at the very least seems destined to give White his pawn back with interest.

|    |         |         |
|----|---------|---------|
| 17 | B×B     | Kt×B    |
| 18 | R–B6    | Kt–Kt6  |
| 19 | B×BP    | Kt–Q5   |
| 20 | Q–R4 *!*| O–O     |

Kt×R would be fatal after P×Kt, Q–B2; 22 Kt–Kt5.

|    |      |
|----|------|
| 21 | R–R6 |

Black's Queen's side is demolished. Unless he can find some counter play his chances are small. The centre is effectively held by White, so the only chance is on the King's wing while so many of White's pieces are away from that side of the board. Note that White's attack has opened up the game. While this helps his attack it will also help Black's counter play.

|    |      |       |
|----|------|-------|
| 21 | ...  | Q–Kt1 *!* |
| 22 | P–B4 |       |

Note that White cannot ignore the threatened attack, e.g. 22 R×RP, Kt–Kt5; 23 P–KKt3, Kt–B6 *ch*; 24 K–Kt2, Kt–Q7 with a dangerous series of threats.

|    |     |         |
|----|-----|---------|
| 22 | ... | P–KKt4 *!* |

All or nothing in this type of situation!

|    |        |           |
|----|--------|-----------|
| 23 | P–K5   | Kt–R4     |
| 24 | P–KKt3 | K–R1      |
| 25 | Q–Q1   | Kt–Kt2    |
| 26 | Q–Kt4  | P×P       |
| 27 | Q×BP   | Kt(Q5)–B4 |

Opening the central file for infiltration by the Rook.

|    |         |        |
|----|---------|--------|
| 28 | Kt–K2   | Kt–R4  |
| 29 | Q–K4    | R–Kt1  |
| 30 | B–Q3    | R–Kt4  |
| 31 | R–B6    | R–Q4   |
| 32 | KR–B1   | K–Kt2  |
| 33 | P–Kt6   | P×P    |
| 34 | R–B7    | P–Kt4  |
| 35 | R(B1)–B6 | Q–Q1  |
| 36 | R–B8    |        |

White is now well on the defensive. To move the Bishop would allow R–Q7.

|    |       |         |
|----|-------|---------|
| 36 | ...   | Q–R4    |
| 37 | Kt–B4 | Kt×Kt   |
| 38 | Q×Kt  | Q–K8 *ch* |
| 39 | B–B1  | Q–K6 *ch* |

Black's counter-attack, so well carried out, has brought its reward. His position is now so good that he can force the transposition into the end-game with a winning advantage.

| | | |
|---|---|---|
| 40 | Q × Q | Kt × Q |
| 41 | R–Q6 | R(Kt4) × KP |
| 42 | R × R | R × R |
| 43 | R–B3 | Kt × B |
| 44 | K × Kt | R–Q8 *ch* |
| 45 | K–K2 | R–KR8 |
| 46 | K–K3 | R × P |
| 47 | P–Kt3 | R–R4 |
| 48 | R–B7 | R–Kt4 |
| 49 | K–B4 | R–Q4 |
| 50 | K–K4 | P–R4 |
| 51 | P–QKt4 | R–Kt4 |
| 52 | K–Q4 | R–Kt5 *ch* |
| 53 | *Resigns* | |

For if 53 K–B5, R–QB5 *ch*.

This game illustrates one very important factor in chess play with which it has not been possible to deal at any great length so far in this book; the question of policy when in an inferior position.

When the game is in a "lost" position, always look round for any counter chances. Never submit tamely with the idea in your head that there is "nothing that can be done about it." Defence, where possible, should be aggressive defence, making it as difficult as possible for your opponent to carry out his plans peacefully and methodically.

If you are in a bad position, there is nearly always something which can be done. Naturally, if your opponent is a good player, that something will not be sufficient to pull the game out of the fire, but for instance, an aggressive counter-attack type of defence will at least give him the chance of making some mistakes.

Very often, too, a player conducting an attack which has given him winning chances, is very loath to consolidate his win, merely by defending himself against your counter-attack, though that may well be the best line of play. On the other hand, if he does so, it may possibly divert sufficient of his forces from the good position he has built up to enable you to free yourself there.

An excellent motto to sum this up would be: Exercise restraint in attack; aggression in defence.

## IN WHICH THERE IS MORE THAN ONE STRATEGY IN THE SAME GAME

In a very large number of games of chess, use can be, and is, made of more than one of the various higher strategies we have already shown.

Many games as we have stated do not show any well defined strategy, such as an attack on a wing running right through the game. However, the reader, having studied this book, should never be at a loss to devise a plan for conducting his game, even though that plan be simple and straightforward, by no means necessarily a disadvantage in a plan.

In the following and concluding game we see an example of a simple combination of strategies—an attack in the centre preceding an attack on the wing. Black sees the possibility of a strong attack on the King's wing. He sees, however, that by combining it with a central thrust this attack will gain considerably in power. In addition this central thrust opens up the position, thus adding to the mobility of the attacking pieces.

GAME NO. 9

*Higher Strategy*

Central thrust combined with a wing attack.

*Weapons Used*

Opening of position by the sacrifice of a piece.
Pin.
Exchanging.
Open file.

|    | *White* | *Black* |
|----|---------|---------|
| 1  | P–Q4    | P–Q4    |
| 2  | P–QB4   | P–QB3   |
| 3  | Kt–QB3  | P–K3    |
| 4  | Kt–B3   | Kt–B3   |

Note that Black does not take the gambit pawn as occurred in Game No. 8.

|    | *White* | *Black* |
|----|---------|---------|
| 5  | P–K3    | QKt–Q2  |
| 6  | Q–B2    | B–Q3    |
| 7  | B–Q3    | O–O     |
| 8  | P–QKt3  | R–K1    |

Black is preparing to free his centre with P–K4.

|    | *White* | *Black* |
|----|---------|---------|
| 9  | O–O     | P–K4    |
| 10 | P×QP    | BP×P    |
| 11 | P×P     | Kt×P    |
| 12 | Kt×Kt   | B×Kt    |

Note how these exchanges have opened up the game.

|    | *White* | |
|----|---------|---|
| 13 | B–Kt2   | |

Black having now got an open game, though White was not compelled to make all the previous exchanges, now plans an attack on the White King's side, initiated by the piece sacrifice B×P *ch*. Before doing so, he decides to thrust on in the centre. This has two objectives. To open up the game still further for his pieces, and to keep White guessing as to whether his intentions are to launch an attack there, or, as happens in the actual game, to branch out on the wing.

13 ...          P–Q5
14 QR–Q1

White elects an indirect defence of the Knight, using the threat of a discovery (if 14 ... P×Kt; 15 B×P *ch*). We shall note later on what would have been the effect of White's taking the pawn with pawn.

14 ...          B×P *ch !*

The reader should note this type of sacrificial attack, which is a common, and often extremely dangerous, one.

15 K–R1

Contrary to custom we propose to digress here for a moment and see the effect of 16 K×B, e.g. 16 K×B, Kt–Kt5 *ch*; 17 K–Kt3 (K–Kt1 would lose immediately after Q–R5, and K–R3 would lose the Queen), Q–B2 *ch*, and at least the piece is regained and White is in a hopeless position.

|    |         |            |
|----|---------|------------|
| 15 | ...     | Kt–Kt5     |
| 16 | P–Kt3   | Q–Kt4      |
| 17 | Kt–K4   | Q–KR4      |
| 18 | K–Kt2   | Kt–K4      |
| 19 | P–B4    | Q–R6 *ch*  |
| 20 | K–B2    | B×KtP *ch* |
| 21 | Kt×B    | Q–R7 *ch*  |
| 22 | K–K1    | Q×Kt *ch*  |
| 23 | R–B2    | Kt–B6 *ch* |
| 24 | K–K2    | R×P *ch*   |

Note now the value of the original pawn-thrust in the centre for Black. Note that, if White had opened up the King's file with 14 P×P, the game would have been over even sooner.

25 K–B1          Q–Kt8 *mate*

## MENTAL DISCIPLINE APPLIED TO CHESS

There is one element which plays its part in every game of

chess, but which has not yet been considered in any detail in this book. We refer to the human element, which can be said to have a vital bearing on the result of almost every contest between two players, and in this respect chess is no exception.

In dealing with such a vast subject the limitations of this book compel us to concentrate on certain aspects only. In any case, we feel sure our readers do not need lessons in chess etiquette, nor do they want merely to be told not to lose heart when in a poor position, or become over-confident in a good one. True, such idealism is hard to achieve, but everyone tries to do so.

### THE FIGHTING ELEMENT IN CHESS

The first aspect on the human side to which we wish to draw the attention of our readers, is the fighting element. A game of chess should be considered as a personal fight between the two Commanders of the pieces, the human players. If you were playing a game against a machine, then, if that machine obtained a winning position, or even obtained some minor strategic advantage, you might as well resign the game. But you will be playing an opponent of flesh and blood, who, even if he does not show them, will be subject to the same fears and liable to the same human errors as yourself. Therefore, you should *not* resign!

Nor is it sufficient merely to prolong the game in the hope that the opposing player will commit some blunder and throw away his advantage. A definite plan of campaign is needed, whether your position is superior, equal, or has deteriorated into an inferior one.

An opponent who has obtained the better position may well find that he has two, three, four, or even five or more ways of turning his advantage into a win. With a poorer position you may have only one or perhaps two lines of action. Remember that only one move can be made at a time, and thus your opponent may be in some difficulty trying to make up his mind which of his many "winning" possibilities to adopt. So by exploiting to the uttermost your solitary line you may unbalance your adversary with his numerous choices.

Thus a demonstration of whatever strength you may have, even if it means a mere exploitation of the manœuvring powers of your pieces against some shadowy or unimportant objective in your adversary's position, should be made so long as you have any such assets left. Such a demonstration may hold no real danger to him at all, but, being human, he may well imagine some hidden terror which is not really there. In the very human battle of life, as in chess, how many of our fears are imaginary ones?

Thus we have our first aspect of the need for mental discipline in chess. In a weaker position to fight off despair and concentrate solely on exploiting whatever assets you have. In a stronger position to examine calmly the threats against you and ignore those that have no basis in fact.

## ADAPTATION OF PLAY TO CHANGING CIRCUMSTANCES

One of the hardest things to discipline is one's natural temperament in the conduct of a game. Some people like to play an attacking type of game; some a close or defensive type. It would be impossible and even undesirable for the reader to attempt to eliminate his particular temperament from his games.

However, one of the commonest causes of failure and disappointment in chess is closely related to this matter of temperament. This factor is the failure to recognize a change in the nature of one's position during the game.

For instance, let us say a player has from the outset been conducting an aggressive attacking game, and reaches a stage when his attack is spent without his having achieved a decisive advantage. It is very often hard to recognize that he will only spoil his position by going on attacking, but perhaps should even switch over to a defensive role. Sometimes, even if this is recognized, it is hard to admit the fact and perhaps harder to carry it out!

Conversely, one may, by circumstances or choice, have been, for most of the game, defending oneself against a strong attack. Finally that attack may be almost over, and the way clear to emerge with a slight superiority in position. Your opponent may at this stage offer you a draw and in sheer relief at having overcome such a deadly attack you may be tempted to accept it.

Again mental discipline is needed. What are the relative merits of the position *now*?

We advise the reader to try to discipline himself rigidly in this respect. Re-examine the position at, or near, any "crisis-point" and for this purpose try to forget entirely what has gone before. Pretend that a friend has given you a diagram of the position, which you are seeing for the first time, and is asking you "What do you think of the game at this point? Who stands better, Black or White?"

To forget what has gone before is so difficult that the advantage you will have over your opponent should you be able to assess a critical position dispassionately and calmly, will be correspondingly great!

## PLIABILITY OF MIND

At the risk of being accused of going back on all that has been written in this book we would say one final thing to our readers.

At all times keep your mind and your plans adaptable to unusual circumstances. Remember that the principles taught in this book constitute knowledge to be put to use by you in the conduct of your games. They are your servants and should not be allowed to become your masters.

If we may be permitted to end this book, as we began, with a military analogy, we suggest that you regard the principles taught in this book as a number of technical experts advising their Commander (the reader). The Commander has the final decision on what must be done; he should always listen to the advice of his experts, but if he considers fit in certain circumstances he should be prepared to over-rule it!

If the battle is won, little more need be said, if lost, the chess Commander lives to fight again, and has the invaluable opportunity of reliving the battle, and searching with the help of those ever present experts, the principles, for the cause of the disaster!

In conclusion, may we wish our patient readers "Good Luck, and better and better chess!"

A CATALOG OF SELECTED
DOVER BOOKS
IN ALL FIELDS OF INTEREST

# A CATALOG OF SELECTED DOVER
# BOOKS IN ALL FIELDS OF INTEREST

CONCERNING THE SPIRITUAL IN ART, Wassily Kandinsky. Pioneering work by father of abstract art. Thoughts on color theory, nature of art. Analysis of earlier masters. 12 illustrations. 80pp. of text. 5⅜ x 8½. 23411-8 Pa. $3.95

ANIMALS: 1,419 Copyright-Free Illustrations of Mammals, Birds, Fish, Insects, etc., Jim Harter (ed.). Clear wood engravings present, in extremely lifelike poses, over 1,000 species of animals. One of the most extensive pictorial sourcebooks of its kind. Captions. Index. 284pp. 9 x 12. 23766-4 Pa. $12.95

CELTIC ART: The Methods of Construction, George Bain. Simple geometric techniques for making Celtic interlacements, spirals, Kells-type initials, animals, humans, etc. Over 500 illustrations. 160pp. 9 x 12. (USO) 22923-8 Pa. $9.95

AN ATLAS OF ANATOMY FOR ARTISTS, Fritz Schider. Most thorough reference work on art anatomy in the world. Hundreds of illustrations, including selections from works by Vesalius, Leonardo, Goya, Ingres, Michelangelo, others. 593 illustrations. 192pp. 7⅛ x 10¼. 20241-0 Pa. $9 95

CELTIC HAND STROKE-BY-STROKE (Irish Half-Uncial from "The Book of Kells"): An Arthur Baker Calligraphy Manual, Arthur Baker. Complete guide to creating each letter of the alphabet in distinctive Celtic manner. Covers hand position, strokes, pens, inks, paper, more. Illustrated. 48pp. 8¼ x 11. 24336-2 Pa. $3.95

EASY ORIGAMI, John Montroll. Charming collection of 32 projects (hat, cup, pelican, piano, swan, many more) specially designed for the novice origami hobbyist. Clearly illustrated easy-to-follow instructions insure that even beginning papercrafters will achieve successful results. 48pp. 8¼ x 11. 27298-2 Pa. $2.95

THE COMPLETE BOOK OF BIRDHOUSE CONSTRUCTION FOR WOOD-WORKERS, Scott D. Campbell. Detailed instructions, illustrations, tables. Also data on bird habitat and instinct patterns. Bibliography. 3 tables. 63 illustrations in 15 figures. 48pp. 5¼ x 8½. 24407-5 Pa. $2.50

BLOOMINGDALE'S ILLUSTRATED 1886 CATALOG: Fashions, Dry Goods and Housewares, Bloomingdale Brothers. Famed merchants' extremely rare catalog depicting about 1,700 products: clothing, housewares, firearms, dry goods, jewelry, more. Invaluable for dating, identifying vintage items. Also, copyright-free graphics for artists, designers. Co-published with Henry Ford Museum & Greenfield Village. 160pp. 8¼ x 11. 25780-0 Pa. $9.95

HISTORIC COSTUME IN PICTURES, Braun & Schneider. Over 1,450 costumed figures in clearly detailed engravings–from dawn of civilization to end of 19th century. Captions. Many folk costumes. 256pp. 8⅜ x 11¼. 23150-X Pa. $12.95

# CATALOG OF DOVER BOOKS

STICKLEY CRAFTSMAN FURNITURE CATALOGS, Gustav Stickley and L. & J. G. Stickley. Beautiful, functional furniture in two authentic catalogs from 1910. 594 illustrations, including 277 photos, show settles, rockers, armchairs, reclining chairs, bookcases, desks, tables. 183pp. 6½ x 9¼. 23838-5 Pa. $9.95

AMERICAN LOCOMOTIVES IN HISTORIC PHOTOGRAPHS: 1858 to 1949, Ron Ziel (ed.). A rare collection of 126 meticulously detailed official photographs, called "builder portraits," of American locomotives that majestically chronicle the rise of steam locomotive power in America. Introduction. Detailed captions. xi + 129pp. 9 x 12. 27393-8 Pa. $12.95

AMERICA'S LIGHTHOUSES: An Illustrated History, Francis Ross Holland, Jr. Delightfully written, profusely illustrated fact-filled survey of over 200 American lighthouses since 1716. History, anecdotes, technological advances, more. 240pp. 8 x 10¾. 25576-X Pa. $12.95

TOWARDS A NEW ARCHITECTURE, Le Corbusier. Pioneering manifesto by founder of "International School." Technical and aesthetic theories, views of industry, economics, relation of form to function, "mass-production split" and much more. Profusely illustrated. 320pp. 6⅛ x 9¼. (USO) 25023-7 Pa. $9.95

HOW THE OTHER HALF LIVES, Jacob Riis. Famous journalistic record, exposing poverty and degradation of New York slums around 1900, by major social reformer. 100 striking and influential photographs. 233pp. 10 x 7⅞. 22012-5 Pa. $10.95

FRUIT KEY AND TWIG KEY TO TREES AND SHRUBS, William M. Harlow. One of the handiest and most widely used identification aids. Fruit key covers 120 deciduous and evergreen species; twig key 160 deciduous species. Easily used. Over 300 photographs. 126pp. 5⅜ x 8½. 20511-8 Pa. $3.95

COMMON BIRD SONGS, Dr. Donald J. Borror. Songs of 60 most common U.S. birds: robins, sparrows, cardinals, bluejays, finches, more—arranged in order of increasing complexity. Up to 9 variations of songs of each species. Cassette and manual 99911-4 $8.95

ORCHIDS AS HOUSE PLANTS, Rebecca Tyson Northen. Grow cattleyas and many other kinds of orchids—in a window, in a case, or under artificial light. 63 illustrations. 148pp. 5⅜ x 8½. 23261-1 Pa. $4.95

MONSTER MAZES, Dave Phillips. Masterful mazes at four levels of difficulty. Avoid deadly perils and evil creatures to find magical treasures. Solutions for all 32 exciting illustrated puzzles. 48pp. 8¼ x 11. 26005-4 Pa. $2.95

MOZART'S DON GIOVANNI (DOVER OPERA LIBRETTO SERIES), Wolfgang Amadeus Mozart. Introduced and translated by Ellen H. Bleiler. Standard Italian libretto, with complete English translation. Convenient and thoroughly portable—an ideal companion for reading along with a recording or the performance itself. Introduction. List of characters. Plot summary. 121pp. 5¼ x 8½. 24944-1 Pa. $2.95

TECHNICAL MANUAL AND DICTIONARY OF CLASSICAL BALLET, Gail Grant. Defines, explains, comments on steps, movements, poses and concepts. 15-page pictorial section. Basic book for student, viewer. 127pp. 5⅜ x 8½. 21843-0 Pa. $4.95

BRASS INSTRUMENTS: Their History and Development, Anthony Baines. Authoritative, updated survey of the evolution of trumpets, trombones, bugles, cornets, French horns, tubas and other brass wind instruments. Over 140 illustrations and 48 music examples. Corrected and updated by author. New preface. Bibliography. 320pp. 5⅜ x 8½. 27574-4 Pa. $9.95

HOLLYWOOD GLAMOR PORTRAITS, John Kobal (ed.). 145 photos from 1926-49. Harlow, Gable, Bogart, Bacall; 94 stars in all. Full background on photographers, technical aspects. 160pp. 8⅜ x 11¼. 23352-9 Pa. $11.95

MAX AND MORITZ, Wilhelm Busch. Great humor classic in both German and English. Also 10 other works: "Cat and Mouse," "Plisch and Plumm," etc. 216pp. 5⅜ x 8½. 20181-3 Pa. $6.95

THE RAVEN AND OTHER FAVORITE POEMS, Edgar Allan Poe. Over 40 of the author's most memorable poems: "The Bells," "Ulalume," "Israfel," "To Helen," "The Conqueror Worm," "Eldorado," "Annabel Lee," many more. Alphabetic lists of titles and first lines. 64pp. 5³⁄₁₆ x 8¼. 26685-0 Pa. $1.00

PERSONAL MEMOIRS OF U. S. GRANT, Ulysses Simpson Grant. Intelligent, deeply moving firsthand account of Civil War campaigns, considered by many the finest military memoirs ever written. Includes letters, historic photographs, maps and more. 528pp. 6⅛ x 9¼. 28587-1 Pa. $11.95

AMULETS AND SUPERSTITIONS, E. A. Wallis Budge. Comprehensive discourse on origin, powers of amulets in many ancient cultures: Arab, Persian Babylonian, Assyrian, Egyptian, Gnostic, Hebrew, Phoenician, Syriac, etc. Covers cross, swastika, crucifix, seals, rings, stones, etc. 584pp. 5⅜ x 8½. 23573-4 Pa. $12.95

RUSSIAN STORIES/PYCCKNE PACCKA3bl: A Dual-Language Book, edited by Gleb Struve. Twelve tales by such masters as Chekhov, Tolstoy, Dostoevsky, Pushkin, others. Excellent word-for-word English translations on facing pages, plus teaching and study aids, Russian/English vocabulary, biographical/critical introductions, more. 416pp. 5⅜ x 8½. 26244-8 Pa. $8.95

PHILADELPHIA THEN AND NOW: 60 Sites Photographed in the Past and Present, Kenneth Finkel and Susan Oyama. Rare photographs of City Hall, Logan Square, Independence Hall, Betsy Ross House, other landmarks juxtaposed with contemporary views. Captures changing face of historic city. Introduction. Captions. 128pp. 8¼ x 11. 25790-8 Pa. $9.95

AIA ARCHITECTURAL GUIDE TO NASSAU AND SUFFOLK COUNTIES, LONG ISLAND, The American Institute of Architects, Long Island Chapter, and the Society for the Preservation of Long Island Antiquities. Comprehensive, well-researched and generously illustrated volume brings to life over three centuries of Long Island's great architectural heritage. More than 240 photographs with authoritative, extensively detailed captions. 176pp. 8¼ x 11. 26946-9 Pa. $14.95

NORTH AMERICAN INDIAN LIFE: Customs and Traditions of 23 Tribes, Elsie Clews Parsons (ed.). 27 fictionalized essays by noted anthropologists examine religion, customs, government, additional facets of life among the Winnebago, Crow, Zuni, Eskimo, other tribes. 480pp. 6⅛ x 9¼. 27377-6 Pa. $10.95

FRANK LLOYD WRIGHT'S HOLLYHOCK HOUSE, Donald Hoffmann. Lavishly illustrated, carefully documented study of one of Wright's most controversial residential designs. Over 120 photographs, floor plans, elevations, etc. Detailed perceptive text by noted Wright scholar. Index. 128pp. 9¼ x 10¾. 27133-1 Pa. $11.95

THE MALE AND FEMALE FIGURE IN MOTION: 60 Classic Photographic Sequences, Eadweard Muybridge. 60 true-action photographs of men and women walking, running, climbing, bending, turning, etc., reproduced from rare 19th-century masterpiece. vi + 121pp. 9 x 12. 24745-7 Pa. $10.95

1001 QUESTIONS ANSWERED ABOUT THE SEASHORE, N. J. Berrill and Jacquelyn Berrill. Queries answered about dolphins, sea snails, sponges, starfish, fishes, shore birds, many others. Covers appearance, breeding, growth, feeding, much more. 305pp. 5¼ x 8¼. 23366-9 Pa. $8.95

GUIDE TO OWL WATCHING IN NORTH AMERICA, Donald S. Heintzelman. Superb guide offers complete data and descriptions of 19 species: barn owl, screech owl, snowy owl, many more. Expert coverage of owl-watching equipment, conservation, migrations and invasions, etc. Guide to observing sites. 84 illustrations. xiii + 193pp. 5⅜ x 8½. 27344-X Pa. $8.95

MEDICINAL AND OTHER USES OF NORTH AMERICAN PLANTS: A Historical Survey with Special Reference to the Eastern Indian Tribes, Charlotte Erichsen-Brown. Chronological historical citations document 500 years of usage of plants, trees, shrubs native to eastern Canada, northeastern U.S. Also complete identifying information. 343 illustrations. 544pp. 6½ x 9¼. 25951-X Pa. $12.95

STORYBOOK MAZES, Dave Phillips. 23 stories and mazes on two-page spreads: Wizard of Oz, Treasure Island, Robin Hood, etc. Solutions. 64pp. 8¼ x 11. 23628-5 Pa. $2.95

NEGRO FOLK MUSIC, U.S.A., Harold Courlander. Noted folklorist's scholarly yet readable analysis of rich and varied musical tradition. Includes authentic versions of over 40 folk songs. Valuable bibliography and discography. xi + 324pp. 5⅜ x 8½. 27350-4 Pa. $7.95

MOVIE-STAR PORTRAITS OF THE FORTIES, John Kobal (ed.). 163 glamor, studio photos of 106 stars of the 1940s: Rita Hayworth, Ava Gardner, Marlon Brando, Clark Gable, many more. 176pp. 8⅜ x 11¼. 23546-7 Pa. $12.95

BENCHLEY LOST AND FOUND, Robert Benchley. Finest humor from early 30s, about pet peeves, child psychologists, post office and others. Mostly unavailable elsewhere. 73 illustrations by Peter Arno and others. 183pp. 5⅜ x 8½. 22410-4 Pa. $6.95

YEKL and THE IMPORTED BRIDEGROOM AND OTHER STORIES OF YIDDISH NEW YORK, Abraham Cahan. Film Hester Street based on Yekl (1896). Novel, other stories among first about Jewish immigrants on N.Y.'s East Side. 240pp. 5⅜ x 8½. 22427-9 Pa. $6.95

SELECTED POEMS, Walt Whitman. Generous sampling from *Leaves of Grass*. Twenty-four poems include "I Hear America Singing," "Song of the Open Road," "I Sing the Body Electric," "When Lilacs Last in the Dooryard Bloom'd," "O Captain! My Captain!"—all reprinted from an authoritative edition. Lists of titles and first lines. 128pp. 5³⁄₁₆ x 8¼. 26878-0 Pa. $1.00

THE BEST TALES OF HOFFMANN, E. T. A. Hoffmann. 10 of Hoffmann's most important stories: "Nutcracker and the King of Mice," "The Golden Flowerpot," etc. 458pp. 5⅜ x 8½. 21793-0 Pa. $9.95

FROM FETISH TO GOD IN ANCIENT EGYPT, E. A. Wallis Budge. Rich detailed survey of Egyptian conception of "God" and gods, magic, cult of animals, Osiris, more. Also, superb English translations of hymns and legends. 240 illustrations. 545pp. 5⅜ x 8½. 25803-3 Pa. $11.95

FRENCH STORIES/CONTES FRANÇAIS: A Dual-Language Book, Wallace Fowlie. Ten stories by French masters, Voltaire to Camus: "Micromegas" by Voltaire; "The Atheist's Mass" by Balzac; "Minuet" by de Maupassant; "The Guest" by Camus, six more. Excellent English translations on facing pages. Also French-English vocabulary list, exercises, more. 352pp. 5⅜ x 8½. 26443-2 Pa. $8.95

CHICAGO AT THE TURN OF THE CENTURY IN PHOTOGRAPHS: 122 Historic Views from the Collections of the Chicago Historical Society, Larry A. Viskochil. Rare large-format prints offer detailed views of City Hall, State Street, the Loop, Hull House, Union Station, many other landmarks, circa 1904-1913. Introduction. Captions. Maps. 144pp. 9⅜ x 12¼. 24656-6 Pa. $12.95

OLD BROOKLYN IN EARLY PHOTOGRAPHS, 1865-1929, William Lee Younger. Luna Park, Gravesend race track, construction of Grand Army Plaza, moving of Hotel Brighton, etc. 157 previously unpublished photographs. 165pp. 8⅞ x 11¾. 23587-4 Pa. $13.95

THE MYTHS OF THE NORTH AMERICAN INDIANS, Lewis Spence. Rich anthology of the myths and legends of the Algonquins, Iroquois, Pawnees and Sioux, prefaced by an extensive historical and ethnological commentary. 36 illustrations. 480pp. 5⅜ x 8½. 25967-6 Pa. $8.95

AN ENCYCLOPEDIA OF BATTLES: Accounts of Over 1,560 Battles from 1479 B.C. to the Present, David Eggenberger. Essential details of every major battle in recorded history from the first battle of Megiddo in 1479 B.C. to Grenada in 1984. List of Battle Maps. New Appendix covering the years 1967-1984. Index. 99 illustrations. 544pp. 6½ x 9¼. 24913-1 Pa. $14.95

SAILING ALONE AROUND THE WORLD, Captain Joshua Slocum. First man to sail around the world, alone, in small boat. One of great feats of seamanship told in delightful manner. 67 illustrations. 294pp. 5⅜ x 8½. 20326-3 Pa. $5.95

ANARCHISM AND OTHER ESSAYS, Emma Goldman. Powerful, penetrating, prophetic essays on direct action, role of minorities, prison reform, puritan hypocrisy, violence, etc. 271pp. 5⅜ x 8½. 22484-8 Pa. $6.95

MYTHS OF THE HINDUS AND BUDDHISTS, Ananda K. Coomaraswamy and Sister Nivedita. Great stories of the epics; deeds of Krishna, Shiva, taken from puranas, Vedas, folk tales; etc. 32 illustrations. 400pp. 5⅜ x 8½. 21759-0 Pa. $10.95

BEYOND PSYCHOLOGY, Otto Rank. Fear of death, desire of immortality, nature of sexuality, social organization, creativity, according to Rankian system. 291pp. 5⅜ x 8½. 20485-5 Pa. $8.95

A THEOLOGICO-POLITICAL TREATISE, Benedict Spinoza. Also contains unfinished Political Treatise. Great classic on religious liberty, theory of government on common consent. R. Elwes translation. Total of 421pp. 5⅜ x 8½. 20249-6 Pa. $9.95

MY BONDAGE AND MY FREEDOM, Frederick Douglass. Born a slave, Douglass became outspoken force in antislavery movement. The best of Douglass' autobiographies. Graphic description of slave life. 464pp. 5⅜ x 8½. 22457-0 Pa. $8.95

FOLLOWING THE EQUATOR: A Journey Around the World, Mark Twain. Fascinating humorous account of 1897 voyage to Hawaii, Australia, India, New Zealand, etc. Ironic, bemused reports on peoples, customs, climate, flora and fauna, politics, much more. 197 illustrations. 720pp. 5⅜ x 8½. 26113-1 Pa. $15.95

THE PEOPLE CALLED SHAKERS, Edward D. Andrews. Definitive study of Shakers: origins, beliefs, practices, dances, social organization, furniture and crafts, etc. 33 illustrations. 351pp. 5⅜ x 8½. 21081-2 Pa. $8.95

THE MYTHS OF GREECE AND ROME, H. A. Guerber. A classic of mythology, generously illustrated, long prized for its simple, graphic, accurate retelling of the principal myths of Greece and Rome, and for its commentary on their origins and significance. With 64 illustrations by Michelangelo, Raphael, Titian, Rubens, Canova, Bernini and others. 480pp. 5⅜ x 8½. 27584-1 Pa. $9.95

PSYCHOLOGY OF MUSIC, Carl E. Seashore. Classic work discusses music as a medium from psychological viewpoint. Clear treatment of physical acoustics, auditory apparatus, sound perception, development of musical skills, nature of musical feeling, host of other topics. 88 figures. 408pp. 5⅜ x 8½. 21851-1 Pa. $10.95

THE PHILOSOPHY OF HISTORY, Georg W. Hegel. Great classic of Western thought develops concept that history is not chance but rational process, the evolution of freedom. 457pp. 5⅜ x 8½. 20112-0 Pa. $9.95

THE BOOK OF TEA, Kakuzo Okakura. Minor classic of the Orient: entertaining, charming explanation, interpretation of traditional Japanese culture in terms of tea ceremony. 94pp. 5⅜ x 8½. 20070-1 Pa. $3.95

LIFE IN ANCIENT EGYPT, Adolf Erman. Fullest, most thorough, detailed older account with much not in more recent books, domestic life, religion, magic, medicine, commerce, much more. Many illustrations reproduce tomb paintings, carvings, hieroglyphs, etc. 597pp. 5⅜ x 8½. 22632-8 Pa. $11.95

SUNDIALS, Their Theory and Construction, Albert Waugh. Far and away the best, most thorough coverage of ideas, mathematics concerned, types, construction, adjusting anywhere. Simple, nontechnical treatment allows even children to build several of these dials. Over 100 illustrations. 230pp. 5⅜ x 8½. 22947-5 Pa. $7.95

DYNAMICS OF FLUIDS IN POROUS MEDIA, Jacob Bear. For advanced students of ground water hydrology, soil mechanics and physics, drainage and irrigation engineering, and more. 335 illustrations. Exercises, with answers. 784pp. 6⅛ x 9¼. 65675-6 Pa. $19.95

SONGS OF EXPERIENCE: Facsimile Reproduction with 26 Plates in Full Color, William Blake. 26 full-color plates from a rare 1826 edition. Includes "TheTyger," "London," "Holy Thursday," and other poems. Printed text of poems. 48pp. 5¼ x 7. 24636-1 Pa. $4.95

OLD-TIME VIGNETTES IN FULL COLOR, Carol Belanger Grafton (ed.). Over 390 charming, often sentimental illustrations, selected from archives of Victorian graphics—pretty women posing, children playing, food, flowers, kittens and puppies, smiling cherubs, birds and butterflies, much more. All copyright-free. 48pp. 9¼ x 12¼. 27269-9 Pa. $5.95

PERSPECTIVE FOR ARTISTS, Rex Vicat Cole. Depth, perspective of sky and sea, shadows, much more, not usually covered. 391 diagrams, 81 reproductions of drawings and paintings. 279pp. 5⅜ x 8½. 22487-2 Pa. $6.95

DRAWING THE LIVING FIGURE, Joseph Sheppard. Innovative approach to artistic anatomy focuses on specifics of surface anatomy, rather than muscles and bones. Over 170 drawings of live models in front, back and side views, and in widely varying poses. Accompanying diagrams. 177 illustrations. Introduction. Index. 144pp. 8⅜ x11¼. 26723-7 Pa. $8.95

GOTHIC AND OLD ENGLISH ALPHABETS: 100 Complete Fonts, Dan X. Solo. Add power, elegance to posters, signs, other graphics with 100 stunning copyright-free alphabets: Blackstone, Dolbey, Germania, 97 more–including many lower-case, numerals, punctuation marks. 104pp. 8⅛ x 11. 24695-7 Pa. $8.95

HOW TO DO BEADWORK, Mary White. Fundamental book on craft from simple projects to five-bead chains and woven works. 106 illustrations. 142pp. 5⅜ x 8. 20697-1 Pa. $4.95

THE BOOK OF WOOD CARVING, Charles Marshall Sayers. Finest book for beginners discusses fundamentals and offers 34 designs. "Absolutely first rate . . . well thought out and well executed."–E. J. Tangerman. 118pp. 7¾ x 10⅝. 23654-4 Pa. $6.95

ILLUSTRATED CATALOG OF CIVIL WAR MILITARY GOODS: Union Army Weapons, Insignia, Uniform Accessories, and Other Equipment, Schuyler, Hartley, and Graham. Rare, profusely illustrated 1846 catalog includes Union Army uniform and dress regulations, arms and ammunition, coats, insignia, flags, swords, rifles, etc. 226 illustrations. 160pp. 9 x 12. 24939-5 Pa. $10.95

WOMEN'S FASHIONS OF THE EARLY 1900s: An Unabridged Republication of "New York Fashions, 1909," National Cloak & Suit Co. Rare catalog of mail-order fashions documents women's and children's clothing styles shortly after the turn of the century. Captions offer full descriptions, prices. Invaluable resource for fashion, costume historians. Approximately 725 illustrations. 128pp. 8⅜ x 11¼. 27276-1 Pa. $11.95

THE 1912 AND 1915 GUSTAV STICKLEY FURNITURE CATALOGS, Gustav Stickley. With over 200 detailed illustrations and descriptions, these two catalogs are essential reading and reference materials and identification guides for Stickley furniture. Captions cite materials, dimensions and prices. 112pp. 6½ x 9¼. 26676-1 Pa. $9.95

EARLY AMERICAN LOCOMOTIVES, John H. White, Jr. Finest locomotive engravings from early 19th century: historical (1804–74), main-line (after 1870), special, foreign, etc. 147 plates. 142pp. 11⅜ x 8¼. 22772-3 Pa. $10.95

THE TALL SHIPS OF TODAY IN PHOTOGRAPHS, Frank O. Braynard. Lavishly illustrated tribute to nearly 100 majestic contemporary sailing vessels: Amerigo Vespucci, Clearwater, Constitution, Eagle, Mayflower, Sea Cloud, Victory, many more. Authoritative captions provide statistics, background on each ship. 190 black-and-white photographs and illustrations. Introduction. 128pp. 8⅞ x 11¾. 27163-3 Pa. $13.95

EARLY NINETEENTH-CENTURY CRAFTS AND TRADES, Peter Stockham (ed.). Extremely rare 1807 volume describes to youngsters the crafts and trades of the day: brickmaker, weaver, dressmaker, bookbinder, ropemaker, saddler, many more. Quaint prose, charming illustrations for each craft. 20 black-and-white line illustrations. 192pp. 4⅝ x 6. 27293-1 Pa. $4.95

VICTORIAN FASHIONS AND COSTUMES FROM HARPER'S BAZAR, 1867–1898, Stella Blum (ed.). Day costumes, evening wear, sports clothes, shoes, hats, other accessories in over 1,000 detailed engravings. 320pp. 9⅜ x 12¼. 22990-4 Pa. $14.95

GUSTAV STICKLEY, THE CRAFTSMAN, Mary Ann Smith. Superb study surveys broad scope of Stickley's achievement, especially in architecture. Design philosophy, rise and fall of the Craftsman empire, descriptions and floor plans for many Craftsman houses, more. 86 black-and-white halftones. 31 line illustrations. Introduction 208pp. 6½ x 9¼. 27210-9 Pa. $9.95

THE LONG ISLAND RAIL ROAD IN EARLY PHOTOGRAPHS, Ron Ziel. Over 220 rare photos, informative text document origin ( 1844) and development of rail service on Long Island. Vintage views of early trains, locomotives, stations, passengers, crews, much more. Captions. 8⅞ x 11¾. 26301-0 Pa. $13.95

THE BOOK OF OLD SHIPS: From Egyptian Galleys to Clipper Ships, Henry B. Culver. Superb, authoritative history of sailing vessels, with 80 magnificent line illustrations. Galley, bark, caravel, longship, whaler, many more. Detailed, informative text on each vessel by noted naval historian. Introduction. 256pp. 5⅜ x 8½. 27332-6 Pa. $7.95

TEN BOOKS ON ARCHITECTURE, Vitruvius. The most important book ever written on architecture. Early Roman aesthetics, technology, classical orders, site selection, all other aspects. Morgan translation. 331pp. 5⅜ x 8½. 20645-9 Pa. $8.95

THE HUMAN FIGURE IN MOTION, Eadweard Muybridge. More than 4,500 stopped-action photos, in action series, showing undraped men, women, children jumping, lying down, throwing, sitting, wrestling, carrying, etc. 390pp. 7⅞ x 10⅝. 20204-6 Clothbd. $25.95

TREES OF THE EASTERN AND CENTRAL UNITED STATES AND CANADA, William M. Harlow. Best one-volume guide to 140 trees. Full descriptions, woodlore, range, etc. Over 600 illustrations. Handy size. 288pp. 4½ x 6⅜. 20395-6 Pa. $5.95

SONGS OF WESTERN BIRDS, Dr. Donald J. Borror. Complete song and call repertoire of 60 western species, including flycatchers, juncoes, cactus wrens, many more–includes fully illustrated booklet. Cassette and manual 99913-0 $8.95

GROWING AND USING HERBS AND SPICES, Milo Miloradovich. Versatile handbook provides all the information needed for cultivation and use of all the herbs and spices available in North America. 4 illustrations. Index. Glossary. 236pp. 5⅜ x 8½. 25058-X Pa. $6.95

BIG BOOK OF MAZES AND LABYRINTHS, Walter Shepherd. 50 mazes and labyrinths in all–classical, solid, ripple, and more–in one great volume. Perfect inexpensive puzzler for clever youngsters. Full solutions. 112pp. 8⅛ x 11. 22951-3 Pa. $4.95

PIANO TUNING, J. Cree Fischer. Clearest, best book for beginner, amateur. Simple repairs, raising dropped notes, tuning by easy method of flattened fifths. No previous skills needed. 4 illustrations. 201pp. 5⅜ x 8½. 23267-0 Pa. $6.95

A SOURCE BOOK IN THEATRICAL HISTORY, A. M. Nagler. Contemporary observers on acting, directing, make-up, costuming, stage props, machinery, scene design, from Ancient Greece to Chekhov. 611pp. 5⅜ x 8½. 20515-0 Pa. $12.95

THE COMPLETE NONSENSE OF EDWARD LEAR, Edward Lear. All nonsense limericks, zany alphabets, Owl and Pussycat, songs, nonsense botany, etc., illustrated by Lear. Total of 320pp. 5⅜ x 8½. (USO) 20167-8 Pa. $6.95

VICTORIAN PARLOUR POETRY: An Annotated Anthology, Michael R. Turner. 117 gems by Longfellow, Tennyson, Browning, many lesser-known poets. "The Village Blacksmith," "Curfew Must Not Ring Tonight," "Only a Baby Small," dozens more, often difficult to find elsewhere. Index of poets, titles, first lines. xxiii + 325pp. 5⅝ x 8¼. 27044-0 Pa. $8.95

DUBLINERS, James Joyce. Fifteen stories offer vivid, tightly focused observations of the lives of Dublin's poorer classes. At least one, "The Dead," is considered a masterpiece. Reprinted complete and unabridged from standard edition. 160pp. 5$^{3}/_{16}$ x 8¼. 26870-5 Pa. $1.00

THE HAUNTED MONASTERY and THE CHINESE MAZE MURDERS, Robert van Gulik. Two full novels by van Gulik, set in 7th-century China, continue adventures of Judge Dee and his companions. An evil Taoist monastery, seemingly supernatural events; overgrown topiary maze hides strange crimes. 27 illustrations. 328pp. 5⅜ x 8½. 23502-5 Pa. $8.95

THE BOOK OF THE SACRED MAGIC OF ABRAMELIN THE MAGE, translated by S. MacGregor Mathers. Medieval manuscript of ceremonial magic. Basic document in Aleister Crowley, Golden Dawn groups. 268pp. 5⅜ x 8½. 23211-5 Pa. $8.95

NEW RUSSIAN-ENGLISH AND ENGLISH-RUSSIAN DICTIONARY, M. A. O'Brien. This is a remarkably handy Russian dictionary, containing a surprising amount of information, including over 70,000 entries. 366pp. 4½ x 6⅛. 20208-9 Pa. $9.95

HISTORIC HOMES OF THE AMERICAN PRESIDENTS, Second, Revised Edition, Irvin Haas. A traveler's guide to American Presidential homes, most open to the public, depicting and describing homes occupied by every American President from George Washington to George Bush. With visiting hours, admission charges, travel routes. 175 photographs. Index. 160pp. 8¼ x 11. 26751-2 Pa. $11.95

NEW YORK IN THE FORTIES, Andreas Feininger. 162 brilliant photographs by the well-known photographer, formerly with *Life* magazine. Commuters, shoppers, Times Square at night, much else from city at its peak. Captions by John von Hartz. 181pp. 9¼ x 10¾. 23585-8 Pa. $12.95

INDIAN SIGN LANGUAGE, William Tomkins. Over 525 signs developed by Sioux and other tribes. Written instructions and diagrams. Also 290 pictographs. 111pp. 6⅛ x 9¼. 22029-X Pa. $3.95

ANATOMY: A Complete Guide for Artists, Joseph Sheppard. A master of figure drawing shows artists how to render human anatomy convincingly. Over 460 illustrations. 224pp. 8⅜ x 11¼. 27279-6 Pa. $10.95

MEDIEVAL CALLIGRAPHY: Its History and Technique, Marc Drogin. Spirited history, comprehensive instruction manual covers 13 styles (ca. 4th century thru 15th). Excellent photographs; directions for duplicating medieval techniques with modern tools. 224pp. 8⅜ x 11¼. 26142-5 Pa. $11.95

DRIED FLOWERS: How to Prepare Them, Sarah Whitlock and Martha Rankin. Complete instructions on how to use silica gel, meal and borax, perlite aggregate, sand and borax, glycerine and water to create attractive permanent flower arrangements. 12 illustrations. 32pp. 5⅜ x 8½. 21802-3 Pa. $1.00

EASY-TO-MAKE BIRD FEEDERS FOR WOODWORKERS, Scott D. Campbell. Detailed, simple-to-use guide for designing, constructing, caring for and using feeders. Text, illustrations for 12 classic and contemporary designs. 96pp. 5⅜ x 8½. 25847-5 Pa. $2.95

SCOTTISH WONDER TALES FROM MYTH AND LEGEND, Donald A. Mackenzie. 16 lively tales tell of giants rumbling down mountainsides, of a magic wand that turns stone pillars into warriors, of gods and goddesses, evil hags, powerful forces and more. 240pp. 5⅜ x 8½. 29677-6 Pa. $6.95

THE HISTORY OF UNDERCLOTHES, C. Willett Cunnington and Phyllis Cunnington. Fascinating, well-documented survey covering six centuries of English undergarments, enhanced with over 100 illustrations: 12th-century laced-up bodice, footed long drawers (1795), 19th-century bustles, 19th-century corsets for men, Victorian "bust improvers," much more. 272pp. 5⅜ x 8¼. 27124-2 Pa. $9.95

ARTS AND CRAFTS FURNITURE: The Complete Brooks Catalog of 1912, Brooks Manufacturing Co. Photos and detailed descriptions of more than 150 now very collectible furniture designs from the Arts and Crafts movement depict davenports, settees, buffets, desks, tables, chairs, bedsteads, dressers and more, all built of solid, quarter-sawed oak. Invaluable for students and enthusiasts of antiques, Americana and the decorative arts. 80pp. 6½ x 9¼. 27471-3 Pa. $7.95

HOW WE INVENTED THE AIRPLANE: An Illustrated History, Orville Wright. Fascinating firsthand account covers early experiments, construction of planes and motors, first flights, much more. Introduction and commentary by Fred C. Kelly. 76 photographs. 96pp. 8¼ x 11. 25662-6 Pa. $8.95

THE ARTS OF THE SAILOR: Knotting, Splicing and Ropework, Hervey Garrett Smith. Indispensable shipboard reference covers tools, basic knots and useful hitches; handsewing and canvas work, more. Over 100 illustrations. Delightful reading for sea lovers. 256pp. 5⅜ x 8½. 26440-8 Pa. $7.95

FRANK LLOYD WRIGHT'S FALLINGWATER: The House and Its History, Second, Revised Edition, Donald Hoffmann. A total revision—both in text and illustrations—of the standard document on Fallingwater, the boldest, most personal architectural statement of Wright's mature years, updated with valuable new material from the recently opened Frank Lloyd Wright Archives. "Fascinating"–*The New York Times*. 116 illustrations. 128pp. 9¼ x 10¾. 27430-6 Pa. $11.95

AUTOBIOGRAPHY: The Story of My Experiments with Truth, Mohandas K. Gandhi. Boyhood, legal studies, purification, the growth of the Satyagraha (nonviolent protest) movement. Critical, inspiring work of the man responsible for the freedom of India. 480pp. 5⅜ x 8½. (USO) 24593-4 Pa. $8.95

CELTIC MYTHS AND LEGENDS, T. W. Rolleston. Masterful retelling of Irish and Welsh stories and tales. Cuchulain, King Arthur, Deirdre, the Grail, many more. First paperback edition. 58 full-page illustrations. 512pp. 5⅜ x 8½. 26507-2 Pa. $9.95

THE PRINCIPLES OF PSYCHOLOGY, William James. Famous long course complete, unabridged. Stream of thought, time perception, memory, experimental methods; great work decades ahead of its time. 94 figures. 1,391pp. 5⅜ x 8½. 2-vol. set.
Vol. I: 20381-6 Pa. $12.95
Vol. II: 20382-4 Pa. $12.95

THE WORLD AS WILL AND REPRESENTATION, Arthur Schopenhauer. Definitive English translation of Schopenhauer's life work, correcting more than 1,000 errors, omissions in earlier translations. Translated by E. F. J. Payne. Total of 1,269pp. 5⅜ x 8½. 2-vol. set. Vol. 1: 21761-2 Pa. $11.95
Vol. 2: 21762-0 Pa. $11.95

MAGIC AND MYSTERY IN TIBET, Madame Alexandra David-Neel. Experiences among lamas, magicians, sages, sorcerers, Bonpa wizards. A true psychic discovery. 32 illustrations. 321pp. 5⅜ x 8½. (USO) 22682-4 Pa. $8.95

THE EGYPTIAN BOOK OF THE DEAD, E. A. Wallis Budge. Complete reproduction of Ani's papyrus, finest ever found. Full hieroglyphic text, interlinear transliteration, word-for-word translation, smooth translation. 533pp. 6½ x 9¼.
21866-X Pa. $10.95

MATHEMATICS FOR THE NONMATHEMATICIAN, Morris Kline. Detailed, college-level treatment of mathematics in cultural and historical context, with numerous exercises. Recommended Reading Lists. Tables. Numerous figures. 641pp. 5⅜ x 8½.
24823-2 Pa. $11.95

THEORY OF WING SECTIONS: Including a Summary of Airfoil Data, Ira H. Abbott and A. E. von Doenhoff. Concise compilation of subsonic aerodynamic characteristics of NACA wing sections, plus description of theory. 350pp. of tables. 693pp. 5⅜ x 8½. 60586-8 Pa. $14.95

THE RIME OF THE ANCIENT MARINER, Gustave Doré, S. T. Coleridge. Doré's finest work; 34 plates capture moods, subtleties of poem. Flawless full-size reproductions printed on facing pages with authoritative text of poem. "Beautiful. Simply beautiful."–*Publisher's Weekly*. 77pp. 9¼ x 12. 22305-1 Pa. $6.95

NORTH AMERICAN INDIAN DESIGNS FOR ARTISTS AND CRAFTSPEOPLE, Eva Wilson. Over 360 authentic copyright-free designs adapted from Navajo blankets, Hopi pottery, Sioux buffalo hides, more. Geometrics, symbolic figures, plant and animal motifs, etc. 128pp. 8⅜ x 11. (EUK) 25341-4 Pa. $8.95

SCULPTURE: Principles and Practice, Louis Slobodkin. Step-by-step approach to clay, plaster, metals, stone; classical and modern. 253 drawings, photos. 255pp. 8⅛ x 11.
22960-2 Pa. $10.95

PHOTOGRAPHIC SKETCHBOOK OF THE CIVIL WAR, Alexander Gardner. 100 photos taken on field during the Civil War. Famous shots of Manassas Harper's Ferry, Lincoln, Richmond, slave pens, etc. 244pp. 10⅝ x 8¼. 22731-6 Pa. $9.95

FIVE ACRES AND INDEPENDENCE, Maurice G. Kains. Great back-to-the-land classic explains basics of self-sufficient farming. The one book to get. 95 illustrations. 397pp. 5⅜ x 8½. 20974-1 Pa. $7.95

SONGS OF EASTERN BIRDS, Dr. Donald J. Borror. Songs and calls of 60 species most common to eastern U.S.: warblers, woodpeckers, flycatchers, thrushes, larks, many more in high-quality recording. Cassette and manual 99912-2 $8.95

A MODERN HERBAL, Margaret Grieve. Much the fullest, most exact, most useful compilation of herbal material. Gigantic alphabetical encyclopedia, from aconite to zedoary, gives botanical information, medical properties, folklore, economic uses, much else. Indispensable to serious reader. 161 illustrations. 888pp. 6½ x 9¼. 2-vol. set. (USO) Vol. I: 22798-7 Pa. $9.95
Vol. II: 22799-5 Pa. $9.95

HIDDEN TREASURE MAZE BOOK, Dave Phillips. Solve 34 challenging mazes accompanied by heroic tales of adventure. Evil dragons, people-eating plants, blood-thirsty giants, many more dangerous adversaries lurk at every twist and turn. 34 mazes, stories, solutions. 48pp. 8¼ x 11. 24566-7 Pa. $2.95

LETTERS OF W. A. MOZART, Wolfgang A. Mozart. Remarkable letters show bawdy wit, humor, imagination, musical insights, contemporary musical world; includes some letters from Leopold Mozart. 276pp. 5⅜ x 8½. 22859-2 Pa. $7.95

BASIC PRINCIPLES OF CLASSICAL BALLET, Agrippina Vaganova. Great Russian theoretician, teacher explains methods for teaching classical ballet. 118 illustrations. 175pp. 5⅜ x 8½. 22036-2 Pa. $5.95

THE JUMPING FROG, Mark Twain. Revenge edition. The original story of The Celebrated Jumping Frog of Calaveras County, a hapless French translation, and Twain's hilarious "retranslation" from the French. 12 illustrations. 66pp. 5⅜ x 8½. 22686-7 Pa. $3.95

BEST REMEMBERED POEMS, Martin Gardner (ed.). The 126 poems in this superb collection of 19th- and 20th-century British and American verse range from Shelley's "To a Skylark" to the impassioned "Renascence" of Edna St. Vincent Millay and to Edward Lear's whimsical "The Owl and the Pussycat." 224pp. 5⅜ x 8½. 27165-X Pa. $4.95

COMPLETE SONNETS, William Shakespeare. Over 150 exquisite poems deal with love, friendship, the tyranny of time, beauty's evanescence, death and other themes in language of remarkable power, precision and beauty. Glossary of archaic terms. 80pp. 5³⁄₁₆ x 8¼. 26686-9 Pa. $1.00

BODIES IN A BOOKSHOP, R. T. Campbell. Challenging mystery of blackmail and murder with ingenious plot and superbly drawn characters. In the best tradition of British suspense fiction. 192pp. 5⅜ x 8½. 24720-1 Pa. $6.95

THE WIT AND HUMOR OF OSCAR WILDE, Alvin Redman (ed.). More than 1,000 ripostes, paradoxes, wisecracks: Work is the curse of the drinking classes; I can resist everything except temptation; etc. 258pp. 5⅜ x 8½. 20602-5 Pa. $5.95

SHAKESPEARE LEXICON AND QUOTATION DICTIONARY, Alexander Schmidt. Full definitions, locations, shades of meaning in every word in plays and poems. More than 50,000 exact quotations. 1,485pp. 6½ x 9¼. 2-vol. set.
Vol. 1: 22726-X Pa. $16.95
Vol. 2: 22727-8 Pa. $16.95

SELECTED POEMS, Emily Dickinson. Over 100 best-known, best-loved poems by one of America's foremost poets, reprinted from authoritative early editions. No comparable edition at this price. Index of first lines. 64pp. 5³⁄₁₆ x 8¼.
26466-1 Pa. $1.00

CELEBRATED CASES OF JUDGE DEE (DEE GOONG AN), translated by Robert van Gulik. Authentic 18th-century Chinese detective novel; Dee and associates solve three interlocked cases. Led to van Gulik's own stories with same characters. Extensive introduction. 9 illustrations. 237pp. 5⅜ x 8½. 23337-5 Pa. $6.95

THE MALLEUS MALEFICARUM OF KRAMER AND SPRENGER, translated by Montague Summers. Full text of most important witchhunter's "bible," used by both Catholics and Protestants. 278pp. 6⅝ x 10. 22802-9 Pa. $12.95

SPANISH STORIES/CUENTOS ESPAÑOLES: A Dual-Language Book, Angel Flores (ed.). Unique format offers 13 great stories in Spanish by Cervantes, Borges, others. Faithful English translations on facing pages. 352pp. 5⅜ x 8½.
25399-6 Pa. $8.95

THE CHICAGO WORLD'S FAIR OF 1893: A Photographic Record, Stanley Appelbaum (ed.). 128 rare photos show 200 buildings, Beaux-Arts architecture, Midway, original Ferris Wheel, Edison's kinetoscope, more. Architectural emphasis; full text. 116pp. 8¼ x 11. 23990-X Pa. $9.95

OLD QUEENS, N.Y., IN EARLY PHOTOGRAPHS, Vincent F. Seyfried and William Asadorian. Over 160 rare photographs of Maspeth, Jamaica, Jackson Heights, and other areas. Vintage views of DeWitt Clinton mansion, 1939 World's Fair and more. Captions. 192pp. 8⅞ x 11. 26358-4 Pa. $12.95

CAPTURED BY THE INDIANS: 15 Firsthand Accounts, 1750-1870, Frederick Drimmer. Astounding true historical accounts of grisly torture, bloody conflicts, relentless pursuits, miraculous escapes and more, by people who lived to tell the tale. 384pp. 5⅜ x 8½. 24901-8 Pa. $8.95

THE WORLD'S GREAT SPEECHES, Lewis Copeland and Lawrence W. Lamm (eds.). Vast collection of 278 speeches of Greeks to 1970. Powerful and effective models; unique look at history. 842pp. 5⅜ x 8½. 20468-5 Pa. $14.95

THE BOOK OF THE SWORD, Sir Richard F. Burton. Great Victorian scholar/adventurer's eloquent, erudite history of the "queen of weapons"—from prehistory to early Roman Empire. Evolution and development of early swords, variations (sabre, broadsword, cutlass, scimitar, etc.), much more. 336pp. 6⅛ x 9¼.
25434-8 Pa. $9.95

THE INFLUENCE OF SEA POWER UPON HISTORY, 1660–1783, A. T. Mahan. Influential classic of naval history and tactics still used as text in war colleges. First paperback edition. 4 maps. 24 battle plans. 640pp. 5⅜ x 8½. 25509-3 Pa. $12.95

THE STORY OF THE TITANIC AS TOLD BY ITS SURVIVORS, Jack Winocour (ed.). What it was really like. Panic, despair, shocking inefficiency, and a little heroism. More thrilling than any fictional account. 26 illustrations. 320pp. 5⅜ x 8½. 20610-6 Pa. $8.95

FAIRY AND FOLK TALES OF THE IRISH PEASANTRY, William Butler Yeats (ed.). Treasury of 64 tales from the twilight world of Celtic myth and legend: "The Soul Cages," "The Kildare Pooka," "King O'Toole and his Goose," many more. Introduction and Notes by W. B. Yeats. 352pp. 5⅜ x 8½. 26941-8 Pa. $8.95

BUDDHIST MAHAYANA TEXTS, E. B. Cowell and Others (eds.). Superb, accurate translations of basic documents in Mahayana Buddhism, highly important in history of religions. The Buddha-karita of Asvaghosha, Larger Sukhavativyuha, more. 448pp. 5⅜ x 8½. 25552-2 Pa. $9.95

ONE TWO THREE . . . INFINITY: Facts and Speculations of Science, George Gamow. Great physicist's fascinating, readable overview of contemporary science: number theory, relativity, fourth dimension, entropy, genes, atomic structure, much more. 128 illustrations. Index. 352pp. 5⅜ x 8½. 25664-2 Pa. $8.95

ENGINEERING IN HISTORY, Richard Shelton Kirby, et al. Broad, nontechnical survey of history's major technological advances: birth of Greek science, industrial revolution, electricity and applied science, 20th-century automation, much more. 181 illustrations. ". . . excellent . . ."–*Isis.* Bibliography. vii + 530pp. 5⅜ x 8¼. 26412-2 Pa. $14.95

DALÍ ON MODERN ART: The Cuckolds of Antiquated Modern Art, Salvador Dalí. Influential painter skewers modern art and its practitioners. Outrageous evaluations of Picasso, Cézanne, Turner, more. 15 renderings of paintings discussed. 44 calligraphic decorations by Dalí. 96pp. 5⅜ x 8½. (USO) 29220-7 Pa. $4.95

ANTIQUE PLAYING CARDS: A Pictorial History, Henry René D'Allemagne. Over 900 elaborate, decorative images from rare playing cards (14th–20th centuries): Bacchus, death, dancing dogs, hunting scenes, royal coats of arms, players cheating, much more. 96pp. 9¼ x 12¼. 29265-7 Pa. $11.95

MAKING FURNITURE MASTERPIECES: 30 Projects with Measured Drawings, Franklin H. Gottshall. Step-by-step instructions, illustrations for constructing handsome, useful pieces, among them a Sheraton desk, Chippendale chair, Spanish desk, Queen Anne table and a William and Mary dressing mirror. 224pp. 8⅛ x 11¼. 29338-6 Pa. $13.95

THE FOSSIL BOOK: A Record of Prehistoric Life, Patricia V. Rich et al. Profusely illustrated definitive guide covers everything from single-celled organisms and dinosaurs to birds and mammals and the interplay between climate and man. Over 1,500 illustrations. 760pp. 7½ x 10⅛. 29371-8 Pa. $29.95

*Prices subject to change without notice.*

Available at your book dealer or write for free catalog to Dept. GI, Dover Publications, Inc., 31 East 2nd St., Mineola, N.Y. 11501. Dover publishes more than 500 books each year on science, elementary and advanced mathematics, biology, music, art, literary history, social sciences and other areas.